More Screams, Different Deserts

More Screams, Different Deserts

Joy and Perseverance for Women in Cross-Cultural Ministry

Sue Eenigenburg

WILLIAM CAREY
LIBRARY

Published by William Carey Library
1605 E. Elizabeth Street
Pasadena, CA 91104 | www.missionbooks.org

Melissa Hicks, editor
Brad Koenig, Beverly Guy, copyeditors
Josie Leung, graphic designer
Santosh Oommen, illustrator
Rose Lee-Norman, indexer

William Carey Library is a ministry of the
U.S. Center for World Mission
Pasadena, CA | www.uscwm.org

Printed in the United States of America

17 16 15 14 13   5 4 3 2 1 BP300

Library of Congress Cataloging-in-Publication Data
Eenigenburg, Susan E.
  More screams, different deserts : joy and perseverance for women in cross-cultural ministry / Sue Eenigenburg.
     pages cm
  Includes bibliographical references.
  ISBN 978-0-87808-537-8
  1. Women in church work--Prayers and devotions. 2. Christianity and culture--Prayers and devotions. I. Title.
  BV4415.E36 2013
  242'.643--dc23

2013015747

To the men and women at Chapel Hill Church
who throughout my life have not only taught me
but also showed me how to love and follow Jesus.
You encourage and inspire me to finish well.

Contents

Foreword

Recently, Sue and I went to see the new release of *Les Misérables* here in South Asia. The theater was nice with reclining easy chairs. Only fifteen people came to this early morning showing. However, the low turnout did not dampen our experience.

The movie, well, moved us. I was thinking, "That was really good!" In contrast, Sue came home and posted on Facebook, "Les Mis was a one tissue plus one napkin plus one sleeve of my sweater tear jerker. Amazing story of mercy, redemption and grace with beautiful music."

For thirty-five years, I have had the privilege of being married to someone who uncovers a touch of humor and spark of divine in ordinary life experiences. Laughter and awe have been my constant companions. I wouldn't have it any other way.

My prayer is that Sue's witty look at daily life will amuse you, and even more, that you will be lifted above your own circumstances to see God's stunning ways behind them.

Each of our kids offered to share something from their own experience growing up as Third Culture Kids (TCKs). I trust their open reflections will provide a helpful backdrop for the rest of the book. And in all things, may God receive the glory!

Don Eenigenburg

Hot 'n' sticky weather . . . New school . . . Language barrier . . .
Ridicule . . . I hate school . . . Persecution of my parents' faith . . .
Trying to fit in . . . What is this food? . . . Loss of friends . . . New
School . . . Two-hour commute to school . . . Loneliness . . . Danger
. . . Persecution of my faith . . . Hot 'n' sticky weather . . . Embassy
kids can get Dr. Pepper, why can't we? . . . Why can't I have a
normal life? . . . Defeat . . . Chaos . . . Self-consciousness . . . Peer-
pressure . . . Hot 'n' sticky weather . . . Confusion . . . Hormones
. . . Cigarettes . . . Babylon 5 every night . . . My stupid family! . . .
Alcohol . . . Who will I date? . . . Who will I marry? . . . Where will
I work? . . . Struggles . . . Will anyone like me? . . . Probably not . . .
Hot 'n' sticky weather . . . GOD

I can take the heat! . . . *Ana bakellum Arabi* . . . Confidence . . .
Quick to adapt . . . God is in control . . . Foreign foods . . . Love to
meet new people . . . Perseverance . . . Gratitude for my parents'
faith . . . Assurance in my faith . . . Patience . . . Determination . . .
Uniqueness . . . Sincerity . . . Care for others . . . Victory . . . Growth
. . . Steadfastness . . . Vigorous . . . My body is a temple . . . My
family is everything to me . . . Adventurous . . . Strong faith . . . God
is with me . . . Emily, my wife . . . Sophie and Stacy, my daughters . . .
Business career . . . GOD

In all of the moments mentioned above it is obvious that God
was working in me. An important connection that isn't so easily
seen, but is nonetheless imperative, was my parents' decision to
value the mission field that is ever present behind closed doors. No
matter the country, culture, criticism, or circumstance, my parents
were faithfully obedient to be Christ's reflection in our home, and
when I was facing difficulties they laid me on the altar of prayer.

Stephen Eenigenburg

I recently met someone at church whom I had not known before,
and he asked me the dreaded question, "So, where did you grow
up?" This is the question I have dreaded ever since I can remember
because of the long, complicated answer and the reaction of "Oh,
this kid is different" showing on their face. This question is followed
by another alienating question, "How was that, growing up overseas

in so many different places?" The look of pity on their face makes me feel like I have been wronged to have moved around and lived in other countries. This is confusing to me because moving every couple of years is just how it was; that was life. I had not known that I was the minority; where I grew up all the other missionary kids (MKs) moved too. Our parents loved us and took care of us, just like parents of non-MKs.

Now that I am older and have kids, I want them to go to other places around the world, experience other cultures, and be able to love people much different than themselves. I have lived in Reading, PA, for fourteen years now. A few years ago I reached the point where I had lived half of my life in the U.S., so I seldom tell people the long saga of where I grew up. I can now just say Reading, PA. But for those who want more details and dig a little deeper, I now have a comeback question for them, "How was it, having to live in the same place your whole life?"

Michael Eenigenburg

When I was little, my family was always different from others. Though it became somewhat normal, we were still different in that we lived in a country with people who looked different from us and who couldn't understand our language. But when we came to America and were among families that we looked more like and spoke like, I realized that we were still different. We were different for more than just cultural reasons; we had different values.

When my friends bemoaned getting yelled at by their parents for getting a 'C', my parents would just ask, "Did you do your best?" If I answered "Yes," then they would say, "That's all you can do then." If I answered, "No," then they would say, "I guess you'll have to make sure you study harder next time."

When my husband and I decided to get married while we were both still in college, I went to my parents and said, "I don't think that we have enough money to live on once we get married." In fact, my whole engagement, I kept waiting for someone to tell us that we weren't ready to get married and that we should wait a bit longer.

Instead, my parents responded, "God will provide." Two years later, when they helped us move into an apartment in a somewhat shady corner of Philadelphia (we went to buy some water at a corner store and found the cash register behind bulletproof glass), my parents told me that this was a great opportunity to learn about an urban culture.

At some point, I realized that I couldn't really shock my parents with any of the things other kids did, because my parents' values were based on the fact that I belonged to God and that he had a plan for me. Their dreams for me didn't involve my being a straight-A student, a successful career woman, or a suburban housewife. Their dreams for me were simple: that I would become a godly woman, find a godly and loving husband, and that we would serve God faithfully. May God grant that my siblings and I teach the same values to the next generation.

Kristi Eenigenburg Digman

Growing up in another culture had its benefits and challenges. I went to a small school with only a couple of other students in my grade. There didn't seem to be many other options for friendships; we became like cousins in a family. Their parents were my aunts and uncles. My mom was always very supportive and allowed me to have sleepovers and go to sleepovers with my friends.

I remember going to school after being infested by the "L" word. I wanted to get sympathy from my friend for all of the torturous treatments my mom had tried on me. As I told her I had lice, she backed away from me in horror, disgusted by the possibility of contamination. As a naturally shy person, my mom was always the only person in my life whom I could tell anything and not worry about how she would react to me. Of course, that time she already knew I had the "L" word!

A short time after I got married and my parents moved overseas, my husband and I decided to get a puppy. I remembered the fun of having my dog Samson (you'll read about him later) when I was younger and I wanted another. My dog Thumper has amplified my appreciation for my mom. I remember being annoyed when my mom would make me walk my dog or clean up after him, but she was the one who had to deal with the dog while I was at school, at sports practices, and at friends' houses. I have quite a list of grievances against my dog Thumper, but I don't ever remember my mom complaining about Samson, and she took care of him while raising four kids dealing with a new culture.

I look up to my mom and all that she has accomplished. She did it with grace and humor. I hope those who read this book can gain some of the wisdom that she has gained and written about in such a clever and inviting way.

Katie Eenigenburg Kunkel

Acknowledgments

I am grateful to God for saving my soul and granting me the privilege of becoming his daughter. His grace is everything to me.

I am thankful for the men and women God has brought around me who have lived out their faith and sought to follow Jesus and share him with the world.

I am thankful for the churches and individuals who have supported us and prayed for us through the years. You are dear to us.

I appreciate my family's support and willingness to let me share my stories, which sometimes revolve around them. My husband, and my children and their families are precious to me.

I am blessed to know God and to be loved by my husband and our growing family.

Introduction

Don and I recently celebrated our twenty-fifth year with Christar. Below is a picture of us when we first got started on our journey of cross-cultural ministry. We were twenty-eight years old, had been married seven years, had two children, and were expecting our third. At the time I thought we were quite mature and ready to take on the lost world for Jesus. Did I mention that I was a bit idealistic and naive?

Young Eenigenburgs

Below is the most recent picture of our family, taken about twenty-five years later. We've served in three different areas of the world, two of which weren't even on our radar when we started out on our journey! All four of our children are now married, and we are delighted to have become grandparents. It didn't take long for the twenty-five years to fly by.

Grown Eenigenburgs

Through years of life and ministry I have learned a few things about both. I've also grown in my walk with God, though I desire to follow him ever more closely and wholeheartedly in the days ahead. I want to continue to passionately pursue God with my whole being until he calls me home.

I think God uses the time we invest in others as a way to keep us close to him. As we share the truths we've learned, we reinforce them into our lives. It keeps things fresh—at least for me, because I tend to have to relearn lessons! Whenever I am preparing for writing or speaking, the Lord has a way of arranging my circumstances so that I need to live out what I am presenting.

In this book I want to share some of what I've learned (and am still learning) with you. I do that best by telling stories and by sharing what I've learned through studying God's word. His word has been central in helping me persevere with joy through some of the stories that God has woven into and around my life.

I also have two questions at the end of each chapter along with a resource in case there is interest in pursuing the topic. One question is for the person who goes across cultures, and the other is for those who help send them.

The stories I'll share are like little slices of my life. The first section focuses on raising kids in a different culture and then examines scriptures that talk about love and perseverance, two qualities that are essential in parenting and cross-cultural ministry.

Stretching spiritually is the theme of the second set of stories. Though it's uncomfortable at times, there is joy in becoming more like Jesus, just knowing he is at work in and through our lives. So we'll intentionally look at some examples of joy lived out through people in the Bible.

It's hard to be involved in cross-cultural work without lots of travel, transitions, and tiredness! The third set of stories revolves around things that have happened to us as we've experienced all three of these challenges . . . sometimes all at once! It is during these times that we really need to remember three of the greatest things mentioned in Scripture: faith, love, and hope.

Last, but not least, are stories centered on several relationships we have as cross-cultural workers. One of the most important lessons I've learned is that my hope and security must rest in God alone and never in another person or group of people. There are two stories in the Old Testament that clearly stand out to me on this topic: the stories of Micah and Jonah provide striking examples of God being our only source of security and hope, and we'll take a look at both of them.

What better way to end a book than by pointing to God alone? It is an even better way to live a life. By God's grace, may it be true of us.

I.
Persevering to Raise TCKs with TLC

Raising children in any culture is difficult. One thing I've learned is that we don't often know the full picture of all that God has done for our children until they are grown and they tell us stories that make our hearts beat faster, even though it is thirty years after the fact! While we were ignorant of some of the circumstances, God was saving our children's lives!

Now that the kids are adults, when we are together I love sitting around the table remembering things that happened when they were children. I thought I knew all the stories. However, now that I've heard "the rest of the story" for several that I thought I knew, I am more thankful than ever that God is omnipresent and omnipotent, because I certainly was not and am not.

We've often told the story of Michael and Kristi being lost on the streets of Cairo when they were eight and five years old. Michael flagged down a taxi, got a ride to the Kentucky Fried Chicken restaurant near our house, and paid an abominably small amount of change for the distance driven. As I shared this account with others, I would say, "God bless that taxi driver. Michael gave him all the money he had, and the taxi driver was so kind not to give him a hard time." We found out a few years ago that Michael had more money; he just didn't want to spend it!

There was the time our girls were out on our fifth-floor balcony with their friend Jennifer. They had tied their two plastic jump ropes together to climb down to the ground. As I stepped onto the balcony,

Jennifer was already over the edge, starting to try to shimmy down the flimsy rope. I got to them just in time to pull her back to safety. Once, as we were talking about that, our oldest son let us know that he used to play on that balcony. He would climb over to the other side and play hold on, let go, grab hold, let go. As he told us, I sat there dumbfounded. Where was I? How did I not know? And even more importantly, why in the world would he do that? He said he thought it had seemed like fun at the time.

We have forgotten our children when I thought Don had them and he thought I had them. When we left our youngest at a restaurant, I called as soon as we got home to ask if she was there. She was. I remember saying, "Tell her we love her and are on our way to pick her up!" It turned out that she was quite pleased because the restaurant manager felt so bad for her that he gave her a free stuffed animal.

Today my children know Jesus and love him. It hasn't been an easy journey for any of us; however, God has been at work. They have each chosen wonderful Christian spouses. They seek to serve him in their jobs and in their homes. They produce the cutest grandchildren I've ever seen.

I, more than anyone in the world, know that this is due to God's grace and mercy. I praise the Lord for his untold mercies and for his watchful care over our children when we weren't there or even aware of what their needs were. Though I am a flawed mother, I am a flawed mother who has an all-knowing, amazingly perfect, totally capable heavenly Father.

Let me tell you a few of our stories . . . or at least the parts I know!

We Should Do That

Ministering in a creative-access country has its challenges. During our first term our children weren't quite sure what their parents did. Because they were so young (all four were under six years old), we weren't sure how to explain to them that we were missionaries but going overseas with a different job. (We didn't use the word "missionary," as the countries where we were going to work didn't allow missionary visas. There was a cultural misunderstanding of the word. Many people often thought of a missionary as not just a religious person, but a political figure with imperialistic goals.) We also didn't do a very good job of helping the children understand so they could explain what we did to people who asked. They knew we moved.

We had been in language study for about one year. Our oldest son, Stephen, was in first grade, where the teacher asked him what his father's job was. He said he didn't know. She tried to help and asked him, "Does your dad read a lot of books?"

"Yes," Stephen replied since he saw him studying almost every evening.

"Does he like old things?"

"Yes," he said as he remembered the different historical places we'd gone to do some sightseeing.

"Is he an archaeologist?" she asked.

"Yes!" our son answered. When we went in for the first parent-teacher conference, we had a hard time understanding why she asked Don about his job in archaeology! She then told us the story of her conversation with our son.

Several years later, after we had finished language school and were in our host country, Dick and Doreen, leaders from our U.S. Sending Center visited us. By then our older kids had a better understanding of Don's role in representing a business while seeking to plant churches. Our younger daughters still weren't sure what we did. We asked Aunt Doreen to share her testimony and pray with our daughters before their bedtime.

Aunt Doreen shared how she came to know the Lord and how she and her husband had traveled around the world telling people about Jesus. Kristi was quite impressed and asked me the next day, "Mom, are Uncle Dick and Aunt Doreen missionaries?" I didn't even know she knew that word, as we rarely used it. We used other terms like "workers" or "macaronis" instead.

"Yes," I replied, "Why do you ask?"

"She told us how she went around the world telling people about Jesus. Hey, we should do that!" She thought we lived at home (in the Middle East) and didn't travel much. We just had lots of friends over and visited them as well.

"Well, honey, we do tell our friends about Jesus." I told her. "That's why we left our home country, invite people to our house, why we are a part of a team, why I go visiting friends when you are at school, why we live here and not where we were born."

"Oh," she said, beginning to understand a little more fully what her parents did.

Questions:

How have you helped your children understand your calling and what you do?

What can churches do to educate the congregation on how to communicate with cross-cultural workers in creative-access countries?

Resource:

A communication guide can be found at http://cma-cmd.nextmeta.com/files/global_ministries/CACCommunicationGuidelinesBrochure2011_785.pdf.

What Happens When Husbands Are Gone

My husband wasn't home. I know it isn't true, but it really does seem as if more unforeseen (and therefore unprepared for) surprises happen when spouses are gone than when they are home!

My two young boys had just arrived home from school. Though they were only in elementary school, they rode a bus with kids their age up through high school-age teens. Sometimes they heard things on that bus that they shouldn't have heard. This was one of those times.

My sons had heard some bad words regarding sex and wanted to find out more about what they had heard. Since I was home, I got the questions. I wasn't really thinking of having this talk until they were older and, well, I just kind of assumed that my husband would talk with them and I would talk with the girls about sex.

I listened as they repeated the words they had heard (oh my!). Their faces showed their disbelief as they said they didn't believe that what the older kids had said about sex could be true. I was thinking, "I'm not ready for this. They aren't ready for this. Where is my husband and how I am going to handle this?" My body, however, was calmly sitting down with them, and my voice said serenely, "Let's talk about what you heard."

Well, we went over the new additions to their vocabulary and we talked about the appropriate words for body parts. I also explained why we don't use crude terms to describe sex when God intended it to be a wonderful demonstration of love that should only happen between a wife and her husband.

We got through the details using correct terminology and a solid theological background, but I think my face turned slightly redder when one of my sons, who was looking at me somewhat shocked and slightly disgusted, asked, "You mean you and dad did that four times?"

I told him that, yes, we had, and then I wasn't sure whether to go on or not. Where was Don anyway? Then I reasoned that I didn't want them to think that the physical side of marriage was only a means to reproduce. So I went ahead and explained that sex isn't just to have babies, but it is a special way husbands and wives show their love to each other.

My other son piped up, "So how often do you and Dad do that?"

Well, I only thought my face was red before. I choked out that there were some things that children didn't need to know.

Thankfully the conversation was waning and they had no more questions, which was good because I was about all out of answers! I ended our time with the statement that if they had anything else like this they wanted to talk about, their dad would be home soon.

They went off to do homework.

I think I just sat on the sofa for a while feeling very weary as I tried to figure out if that went well or not. Did I miss anything important, say too much or too little? Were they supposed to ask questions like these at such a young age? I had a lot more questions after answering some of theirs.

The biggest one was, "How could I arrange for my husband to be home the next time this topic came up?"

Questions:
What can you and your spouse do to prepare for questions from your children about sex?

How can churches and supporters effectively minister to the TCKs when they are on home assignment and when they are overseas?

Resource:
David C. Pollock and Ruth E. Van Reken, *Third Culture Kids: Growing Up among Worlds* (Boston: Brealey, 2009).

The "L" Word

When my kids were little I received the dreaded call from their school. One of them had lice, and as a result they all became contaminated. This was a new experience, and I wasn't sure what to do. I felt embarrassed, like I should have been able to prevent them from getting lice.

We washed their hair and then read that washing hair with lice only produces cleaner lice.

We now had clean lice.

We cut their hair. With the boys this was quite effective as we could cut most of their hair off. With the girls this was not a good solution. We had two boys with really short haircuts and two girls with shorter hair . . . and lice. I read some more.

Hmm. Vaseline could smother lice. I was supposed to put Vaseline through their hair and then wrap their heads with plastic wrap for several hours. This is easier said than done. But they sat still as I applied a very large jar of Vaseline on each of their heads. I then wrapped their heads with plastic wrap. The plastic wrap kept sliding off and I kept sliding it back on and then washing the grease off my hands.

The girls had greasy hair for a week, even after washing it time and time again.

We now had clean, greasy lice.

A friend recommended a product you could buy at the store that came with a fine-tooth comb for nit-picking. (I finally understood what the phrase "nitpicky" meant, more fully than I cared to know!) I bought the stuff, put it in their hair, and proceeded to spend hours with the comb trying to find all the nits and get rid of the lice.

We now had clean, greasy lice that were apparently experts in camouflage and remained undetected.

We regularly washed sheets and pillowcases in hot water using our semiautomatic washing machine (which I think should really be called semimanual!).

We got so tired of trying to get rid of lice, and so frustrated that we couldn't succeed, that we hated even saying the word "lice." Thus we simply called them the "L" word. I hated them and felt defeated. How can you fight against such tiny creatures that, though they only live about a month, produce seven to ten eggs each day? These eggs hatch, and it only takes ten days for them to become adults and continue the cycle. Lice don't fly. They don't leap. But they are transferred via people or objects. So our girls couldn't spend the night at their friends' houses, and their friends didn't want to stay with us. I didn't even want to stay with us!

We had clean, greasy, camouflaged lice that were seriously affecting all our lives. We were tempted to shave the girls' heads. We finally went to the doctor seeking a miracle. He wrote a prescription for some very strong medicine after making sure that I had tried everything else I could to get rid of them. I was desperate to convince him that we had and that we really, really needed this miracle drug.

We picked up the medicine. We put it in their hair. We got nit-picky with the comb. We washed the sheets. We did everything in our power to make the "L" go away.

And finally, there was sweet success. Not one "L" was found, and we were "L" free. To this day, we still don't use the full word for those vermin. In our family, it's considered a dirty word which we never say!

Not every family considers "lice" a dirty four-letter word that is forbidden, but if they are ever infested, I think they might agree with us!

Questions:

What has your family had a difficult time battling? What are some resources that you have found to help?

How can churches and supporters find and share resources for workers that deal with anything from eliminating lice to delivering a baby?

Resources:

David Werner, *Where There Is No Doctor: A Village Health Care Handbook*, 2nd ed., with Carol Thuman and Jane Maxwell (Berkeley, CA: Hesperian, 2011); and A. August Burns et al., *Where Women Have No Doctor: A Health Guide for Women* (Berkeley, CA: Hesperian, 2012). These are available as free downloads at http://hesperian.org/books-and-resources.

What Can I Say?!

When God calls us into the ministry, it means he is also calling our children. Parents aren't the only ones who go through culture stress, language learning, and feeling as if we don't belong. Even though our children were quite young when we first left to go overseas, they still experienced culture stress, not only in our host country but in our home country. They learn and adapt, but the process is not without its challenges.

When one of our sons was a young teen, he was trying to think of what to get his dad for his birthday. We thought about it and came up with the idea of windshield wipers. Our car didn't have any and didn't normally need them for about eleven months out of the year. But there was that one month when they would be quite useful! So the question came, "Mom, how do you say 'windshield wipers' in Arabic?"

I didn't know the word but told him he could walk to a garage, use hand motions and ask if they had any of "those" that did "that" for a car. For some odd reason he had no desire to make his hands act like windshield wipers! Hmm. So I asked a friend how to say it. She said they were called *mesahat*—which is really quite interesting because it comes from the root word meaning "to anoint." So Christ is the Messiah or *Meseeh* because he is the anointed one. So anyway, enough of a language lesson, I told him what the word was and he went to a nearby garage.

A little later he came home empty-handed. It turns out he messed up. He added one extra sound—just one extra vowel that changed the meaning of what he said. Instead of asking for windshield wipers he asked for Christian women. Oh no! As soon as he said he had requested *Mesahiat*, I knew what had happened and explained about that extra vowel. I said he could just go back and use the right word. He said he didn't want to *ever* go there again and that he would come up with something else to get his dad.

Learning the language can be difficult for everyone. We all make mistakes that make us wish we had kept our mouths closed. Then there are words we can say correctly but wish we didn't have to use!

The word for "winter" in Arabic is *shita*, and I had a very hard time saying this word. I would intentionally say it in a way that didn't sound like an American cuss word. The teacher would then correct me and repeat it for me, stressing each syllable to show me how it is supposed to sound: *shit' a, shit' a.* I finally figured it was easier just to say it the correct way and to hope that winter passed quickly!

Soon we were reading in Arabic, and I was in big trouble as I began a sentence that sounded exactly like the word "enema." I couldn't stop laughing, as what I was saying, thinking, and reading were radically different concepts!

In language study I just couldn't seem to get away from words that were bad in English or that reminded me of bodily functions!

Years of language study were valuable as we began to have the wonderful ability to communicate the gospel in another language. It was thrilling to share it with my next-door neighbor who had never heard it before! Don began teaching and mentoring future leaders and pastors.

However, we never quit learning! Don's send-off for his friend, who was emigrating to Canada, is my favorite blooper. He meant to say, "May God grant you success," but due to a little mix-up in letters he said, "May God put you to death."

Thankfully his friend knew what Don meant and is hopefully enjoying a long life in Canada!

Questions:
How does your learning style affect your language studies?

What plans are in place to regularly encourage cross-cultural workers in their first term as they deal with culture stress and language study?

Resource:
A short video clip by John Piper about learning a new language: http://www.brigada.org/2012/11/25_9999.

All-American Baseball
. . . Kind Of

We were home on furlough, living with my parents for a short time. The grass was wonderfully green, and the kids were able to play outside, shooting baskets or playing catch. It felt so "normal" to me. I remember playing kickball or spud outside with friends in the field across the street as a child. The country road was quiet, and playing outside on warm summer evenings seemed so . . . American. We grilled outside, went for walks in local parks, and enjoyed simply hanging out with family.

What was normal for me was unusual for my kids. They were growing up in a city of 15 million people. Streets were crowded; rabid dogs and herds of woolly sheep, goats, water buffalo, and even camels roamed the streets in between cars, buses, bikes, and taxis. To play safely we had to go to a special park or club. Going outside to play without cars honking or animals wandering was something they hadn't experienced much.

One day our boys went outside to play catch. They weren't out there long before they came inside looking guilty. "Um, Mom, we were playing catch, and the baseball broke the neighbor's window."

I was thrilled! (The boys were surprised at my response!) I never thought our kids would get to do something so "American." It was like a scene out of *Leave It to Beaver*. I tried not to act too elated in front of the children. After all, this was a serious thing. They needed to go over to the neighbor, apologize, and offer to pay for the damages.

This was way cool! Calmly, we walked over to the neighbor's house and knocked on the door. A guy I went to high school with opened the door. I guess I wasn't as calm as I thought, and I just couldn't stop smiling as we explained what happened. He must have thought it was rather strange for a mother to be so excited about a broken window. But that's because he thought it was a normal event and not something special. I'm not sure what my sons thought since they probably had assumed they would be in trouble! The neighbor said he would get it fixed and let us know how much it cost.

We went back to my parents' home, and everything was wonderfully resolved, exactly like an episode in *Leave It to Beaver*, except I wasn't wearing pearls. Plus, in just a few short months we were headed back to our host city where no one really played baseball, almost everyone lived in apartment buildings, and no one knew who Beaver was! How many chances would I have to be in a situation like those depicted by my old favorite television shows?

Surprisingly, not too long after that, our boys actually had the chance to play baseball as someone started a Little League program back in our host country. They signed up, learned the rules, and got to play baseball. They loved it.

The only difference from the baseball games they would have played in the States was the herd of goats grazing in the outfield!

Questions:

What are ways we can help our kids adjust during entry and reentry into their different cultures?

Reverse culture shock can hit returning families. How can a church family help returning workers?

Resources:

Ron and Bonnie Koteskey, *Coming "Home": The Reentry Transition*, free download at http://www.missionarycare.com/reentry.htm. There is also a downloadable resource for children ages six to twelve with a guide for parents.

It's Only an Earthquake

I was sitting on the floor talking with my friend on the telephone. My four-year-old daughter was playing nearby. As we were chatting, I noticed our chandelier beginning to swing and saw books falling off of our shelves. The building started to shake, and the floor was rolling like the waves of the ocean. A vase crashed to the floor. "My building is shaking," I said to my friend.

"Mine is too," she replied.

My daughter—her big, brown eyes round with fright—came to sit on my lap. "What's going on?" I asked my friend.

"I think it's an earthquake," she answered.

I held my daughter close as I said as calmly as I could, "Don't worry, honey. It's only an earthquake."

Eventually the shaking stopped and the chandelier quit swinging. My friend and I hung up to see how things were in our neighborhoods.

As I stepped out into the hall, I realized all of our neighbors had run outside. I wondered if my husband and other three children were okay and where they were. As it turned out, my kids were in a taxi on their way home from school and didn't feel a thing. They couldn't figure out why everyone was running out of buildings and why there were so many people gathered together on the streets. My husband and a coworker had just finished praying and, similar to Acts 4:31, "when they had prayed, the place where they had gathered together was shaken" (NASB).

As news reports came in, we realized that the earthquake measured 5.9 on the Richter scale, and the final reports recorded 552 dead; 9,929 injured; 5,000 homes destroyed; and over 11,000 homes damaged.

Looking back at such a terrible event, I wondered at the calm with which I assured my daughter, "It's only an earthquake." Part of it might have been shock or a state of denial as I had never been in an earthquake before, but one was happening that very minute. Part of it was that, no matter how enormous or dreadful the event, I realized God's presence and peace are always available when we trust him. Part of it was simply the desire to reassure my daughter that everything would be okay.

Today when a crisis occurs, I like to think back and remember confidently telling my daughter, "It's only an earthquake." Whatever happens, nothing is bigger than God.

"It's only" is a good way to describe anything we cannot handle or we are afraid of, because it reminds us how small it is in comparison to our Almighty God.

Questions:
What is an "it's only" in your life that you need to recognize in light of who God is?

Does your church have plans to help workers who face serious health issues, natural disaster, or personal crisis? What can be done to lay a foundation for working with the sending agency to help quickly in times of need?

Resource:
Crisis Consulting International (http://www.cricon.org) holds training seminars and helps with risk assessments.

Where Is the Museum?

I learned early on that kids and boredom don't go well together.
After the routine of school, we had to have some activities planned
out so that the kids had just enough structure to enjoy the summer.
We had days when we went swimming and days with reading and
going to the library, and one day each week we did some sightseeing

I planned to take my kids to a different museum each week.
There are advantages to living in a city that is thousands of years
old! I looked through a local magazine and discovered a list of
museums. It was hot and sunny every day. The kids weren't really
thrilled about our adventures, but I led the way with forced enthusi-
asm, mediating arguments with as much optimism as I could handle.
We were already sweaty and tired by the time we settled into a taxi
that would take us to our destination.

We went to a post office museum, a railroad museum, an ento-
mological museum. I must admit that one was my sons' favorite but
my least favorite. There was dead bug after dead bug after dead bug,
which in hindsight, I guess, is much better than live ones! Who knew
there were so many different kinds of beetles!

The famous Egyptian Museum was my favorite. We saw King
Tut and all manner of ancient mummies and sarcophaguses. It is the
only museum in the world that I could have roamed for days. I think
we toured it in about an hour!

That summer we saw so much history and learned so much
about the culture in which we were living. We saw the Coptic
museum and learned about the history of Christianity in Egypt. The
ethnological museum was filled with ancient relics and artifacts.
We were fascinated; well one of us was! The children tagged along,

sometimes reluctantly, but sometimes managing to enjoy themselves as well.

One museum we never found. Another museum was off the beaten path. We got out of the taxi and walked up to the guard asking about the museum. "You want to see this museum?" he asked in an amazed voice. I replied that we did. The kids didn't say anything. Maybe they were hoping he wouldn't let us in and that we would have to change our plans! He jumped to his feet and yelled, "Hey Ahmed, where is the key?"

The guard led the way for us after finally finding the key, but the whole way through he used a feather duster to clean off the exhibits as we followed behind!

I guess that museum wasn't anyone's favorite!

Questions:
What are some activities you can plan with your children in the country where you live?

How can churches and supporters help TCKs learn more about American history, and how can TCKs be encouraged to share about the culture in which they live with kids living in America?

Resources:
For MK reentry seminar information: http://www.barnabas.org/reentry/who.php. For other opportunities for college-age children: http://www.mukappa.org/.

A Mother's Sacrifice

We could find some chocolate in our host city, but not Reese's Peanut Butter Cups or Hershey bars or Nestlé's chocolate chips. My parents were kind enough to send us care packages filled with all kinds of goodies. We would ration one bag of chocolate chips to make three batches of chocolate-chip cookies rather than using them all for just one batch as the recipe recommended. We could hardly imagine using the whole package all at once! Rationing became a habit.

My teenage niece was visiting us for Christmas and asked if she could make some cookies. I said yes. I happened to come into the kitchen just as she was pouring the *entire* bag of chocolate chips into the dough for just one batch of cookies. Before I could stop myself I yelled, "What are you doing?"

She was stunned and stammered, "I'm making cookies. I asked if I could." I had forgotten to tell her about rationing. By the way, her cookies were amazingly good and chocolaty! Still, rationing remained a way of life for anything that was hard to find—from Ziploc bags to candy from home. (But especially candy from home!)

It was my job as the mother to protect my children from too much sugar, and I took that job very seriously. Therefore it was part of my sacrificial duty to eat most of the chocolate! We would open the care package, and I would dole out amounts appropriate for the children; then I would put the rest away to enjoy at my leisure— usually in secret or after they were in bed. They went to bed happy that they could have some candy, and I went to bed full!

There were other things that were hard to find in our city. Apples were rare, and those you could sometimes find were costly. One year for Christmas I asked for apples and hoped to get some as a gift.

On Christmas morning we opened our packages and (yes!) I got a kilo of Granny Smith apples!

As I cut my apples into pieces to eat, I realized I shouldn't be selfish. I should share. Apples were healthy and children should eat them. And so I asked a question—a question that continues to haunt me long after my children have become adults—"Who wants to chew the core?" And the amazing thing is that there was a chorus of "Me! Me!" I would kindly dole out the core for the designated one to chew on and then discard. Everyone was happy!

As my children grew and care packages would arrive, we would open them and ooh and aah over all that was inside. The day finally came when my oldest son said, "Mom, why don't you divide up all the candy into piles so we each have our own." I looked over at my cunning child and primly told him that he could trust his mother.

He replied, "With everything but chocolate." That ended (for the most part) my selfless sacrifice to protect my children from too much sugar. We began to divide the spoils and, with some supervision, they managed to make it last quite a while—maybe even longer than mine!

I'd like to think that memory has faded into history for our family. However, to this day, whenever someone in my family eats an apple and I'm around, the question will inevitably pop up again, "Do you want to chew on the core?"

Questions:

How can we teach our children to share when it is so easy to be selfish?

What are the custom regulations and possible delivery problems when sending a care package? Sometimes packages don't reach the recipient or things are stolen. Sometimes receiving the package costs more than what the package is worth! Ask workers what they miss, and send them a gift if it is feasible.

Resources:
Instructions on preparing international shipments: https://www.usps.com/ship/prepare-international-shipments.htm and http://www.fedex.com/us/service-guide/our-services/international/index.html.

The Birth

It was almost time to have our fourth baby. We had been living in our host country about a year and a half. The hospital was too far to walk to, and we didn't have a car. We planned to take a taxi. We also planned for someone to come and stay with the older three kids while we went to the hospital.

I had just visited the doctor, and he said he would see me that night or the next day, as I had been having contractions off and on for several days. Early the next morning a friend came over to watch the kids so we would be ready to go to the hospital. She stayed. And stayed. The contractions stopped. Don and I went for a walk. We bought a newspaper and some cookies for the guests who would come after we had the baby. We got home. No contractions. My friend needed to go, and I called another friend who was supposed to come over; I told her not to come since nothing was happening. I was waving goodbye to one friend and talking on the phone to another when my water broke. I asked the friend on the phone to please come and the other one to wait just a little longer.

I went into the bathroom to dry off and change my clothes. Then it struck me. What happens if I leak water in the taxi? It's not like it's something I could control. How embarrassing would that be! What would I say to the driver? I was so worried about ruining his seat that I didn't have time to concentrate on the contractions! As soon as we got to the hospital and I stepped out of the taxi, more water gushed onto the sidewalk. I was thrilled to not have to explain to the taxi driver why his seat was wet! However, without that to think about anymore, I realized that my contractions were coming fairly regularly.

Once we registered we got into the elevator to take us up to the labor and delivery floor. The elevator operator said, "I hope it is a boy." Now *that* made me mad. And I was probably not in the best frame of mind at that point to handle a confrontation! Who was he to say it should be a boy! I wanted a baby—boy or girl. Why did he have to say that? Thankfully we arrived at the floor before I did or said something I would regret later.

The nurses didn't know if I was really in labor. Seriously? My pants were soaked and my contractions were regular. We insisted they check and call the doctor. I was almost ready to deliver. The doctor arrived. Kathryn Linzy was born. We were thrilled to have a daughter.

Where would that elevator operator be if his mother had been a son? He wouldn't be, at all!

Sons and daughters are all gifts from God.

Questions:

Does your host culture view boys and girls differently? If so, what are ways we can show value to both sexes?

Recognizing the harassment that many female workers and their daughters can face living abroad, what counseling or mentoring help can you have available specifically for them?

Resource:

The two-part article, "Raising Radiant Daughters": http://parentingasyougo.wordpress.com.

One of the Differences between Us and Hamsters

We got our son a guinea pig for his birthday. He was so excited. Then he was very sad; after only a few days the guinea pig was dead. We went to the store to get another guinea pig. That one also died in less than a week. We realized we must not be guinea pig people.

So we went to the pet store and came back with a hamster. We named her Miss Brown. She was adorable, and all the kids liked her. After several days we noticed we weren't seeing her as often. Was she gaining weight? Why was she was hiding under her construction of a pile of newspapers at one end of the cage? It was after counting eleven baby hamsters that we changed her name to Mrs. Brown.

We weren't sure what we were going to do with twelve hamsters, but the hamsters themselves took matters into their own hands. One morning our son yelled for us to come. We ran into the living room and he said, "They're eating the littlest one!" Oh no. Wasn't I feeding them enough? I didn't know hamsters did this. Yuck! This was particularly traumatic for our son who lifted tear-filled eyes and pro-claimed, "We wouldn't do that to Katie." Katie is his youngest sister.

Yes, thankfully there is a difference between people and hamsters!

I started feeding them more and never let them run out of things to eat. As the remaining ten baby hamsters grew, I started reading up on hamsters and tried to find out when they start reproducing. I discovered it wasn't long. So we got another cage so we could have a home for the girls and a home for the boys. I also had to read up on how to tell the difference between boy hamsters and girl hamsters. It was hard as they were so tiny and covered with fur. The book said that the female would have three little holes and the males would have two. So, one at a time I lifted them up and counted "one, two, three" or simply "one, two." Glad to have that settled and the sexes segregated, we began contacting friends to see if anyone would like a new pet hamster free of charge!

A little while later we again heard our son calling frantically for us to come into the living room. Afraid of recurring cannibalism, we came quickly. No, they weren't depleting their population—they were actually trying to increase their number! Oops! I had missed one of the boys and had him in with the girls. I rapidly rectified that situation and was now certain we had all the boys in one cage and all the girls in another.

After contacting friends and friends of friends (friends we hoped would stay our friends), we eventually gave all of the hamsters away with only Mrs. Brown staying with us.

She must have missed her little ones because, though I am sure I was giving her enough to eat, Mrs. Brown soon passed away.

It was then we decided, pretty much unanimously, that we weren't hamster people either!

Questions:
What are some ways you have helped your children deal with death, whether that of a loved one or a pet?

When a worker faces the death of a loved one in her home country, what can churches and supporters do to help comfort her?

Resource:
Pat Schwiebert and Chuck DeKlyen, *Tear Soup: A Recipe for Healing after Loss*, 5th ed. (Portland, OR: Grief Watch, 2005).

A Dangerous Prayer

It was Valentine's Day, 1998. I was picking up my children from
school. My older son and his girlfriend had just broken up. Though
in the car, he wanted to go talk with her and raised his voice to tell
me to stop the car. I, however, did not pull over as I asked him to not
yell. He opened the door and started to get out anyway. I began to try
to stop, but it was too late.

In one fell swoop I lost any hope of being named mother of the
year or driver of the year. I ran over my son's foot. He was limping
as he ran across the field to the school to talk with his former girlfriend. I stayed on the road and drove as quickly as I could to the
same place. My daughters were whimpering in the back seat. I was
near tears myself but trying to stay calm. I picked him up at the
school and picked up my other son who had planned to go out with
friends. I announced that we were all going home.

My hands were shaking as I tried to fit the key into the lock
to enter our apartment. I think the kids went to their rooms. I only
remember going into our bedroom where I fell, sobbing, onto the bed
and wept until I thought I could weep no more. I knew I needed to
call Don and ask him to come home. He took our son to the hospital
for X-rays where the doctor said his foot was fine (thank God) and
nothing was broken.

What kind of mother runs over her own son? I cannot describe
to you the guilt and anguish that I experienced. To this day the mere
thought of it brings tears to my eyes. I should have known that he was
too upset. I should have been better prepared. I should have known to
stop. Aren't mothers supposed to protect their children? I felt like a
lousy mother and felt judged by others to be a bad mom as well.

It was a tumultuous time in our son's life. It seemed he was being pulled in many directions. The world was battling for his soul, but the Lord had laid a previous claim. We encouraged him in his spiritual life, but he also had friends who encouraged him to enjoy what the world had to offer.

We chose to fast and pray for him every Monday. We did not know this would become a practice for several years. By God's grace, we continued to entrust him to the Lord and believe that he would choose the Lord over all else. I remember that during one prayer time the Lord seemed to ask me a question: "Sue, would you like a child who merely goes through the motions and doesn't know me or a child who goes through a time of trial but in the end comes close to me?" What was more important to me? To look like a good mother by having children who simply acted the part of believers or to possibly appear like a bad mother to others while my children came to really know him. The choice was clear. My heartfelt desire was for each of my children to really know the Lord.

There were times I felt afraid. I sensed that I was failing. I felt alone. God provided a group of mothers that I met with weekly. There I could cry, be open, share, complain, say whatever I needed to say, and know that it would by no means ever leave that room. I would be loved no matter what, would never be judged, and would always be prayed for faithfully.

Through this difficult time, by God's grace, I determined to always be proud of my children, to let them know I was on their side, their number one fan. I also let them know that I was praying for them.

One night I was talking with my teenage son and told him, "I am praying for you. I am asking that God will do whatever it takes to make you a man after God's heart, the man he wants you to be." He looked at me, somewhat taken aback, and said, "That's a really dangerous prayer."

I said, "I know, but it's worth it."

And it has been.

Questions:
What are some "dangerous" prayers you are praying for your children or loved ones?

What can be done to help churches pray more fervently for the cross-cultural workers they support? What part does fasting play in praying fervently?

Resource:
"30 Ways to Pray for Missionaries":
http://www.encompassworldpartners.org/component/content/
article/46/603-30-ways-to-pray-for-missionaries.

II.
A Deeper Look at Love and Perseverance

Now that our four children are grown and I've had time to ponder raising them, I realize that there are several key ingredients in parenting, whether the children are TCKs or not.

1. We need to walk steadfastly with the Lord, continually growing in our love for him.
2. We need to loyally and passionately love each other as the parents of these gifts from God.
3. We need to faithfully and constantly love our children. We must consistently discipline them and encourage them with strength, tenderness, and love.

These words are so easy to type and so hard to practice!

I believe that children are very forgiving when they know they are loved. As our family sits around the dinner table and they reminisce about their childhood, we are all aware that none of us is perfect. We made mistakes. Our kids made mistakes. But at the end of the day we always knew we were loved by God and by each other.

There was a love that, by God's grace, abided. It persevered through temper tantrums, running away from home, and bickering with others . . . and that was just me! Being a mother has been one of the most challenging and rewarding roles of my life. There were times I didn't know if I or the children would make it. But we did!

In all of life there is one quality that speaks louder to me than any words. It hangs in there when other characteristics might waver. It is the value of perseverance. Persisting through disappointments, trials, and challenges communicates godly love that never fails. As we grow in perseverance, the love that we experience and share perseveres and grows as well.

Of course we cannot love like that on our own. It is a gift from God. This gift isn't inert, though: it grows and flows as we exercise consistency and patient endurance. Love and perseverance are two qualities that both cross-cultural workers and mothers must be developing to fulfill God's calling on our lives—loving and persevering not just as families but as teams in cross-cultural settings.

Let's take some time to examine love and perseverance, first by examining in depth the truth found in 2 Thessalonians 3:5: "May the Lord direct your hearts into God's love and Christ's perseverance." We will then look at other scriptures that give truth to strengthen us in perseverance.

Love

Don and I recently celebrated our thirty-fourth wedding anniversary. We went out to celebrate and, as we looked back through our years together, it became obvious to us that we have been and will be in this relationship for the long haul. Our love has waned at times but, by God's grace, our commitment to stay together has seen us through some rough patches. I almost ran away from home several times. I learned how to voice my needs rather than expect Don to know about them intuitively. We've disappointed each other. We've also laughed together and played together. Exploring different countries and meeting new friends have enriched our relationship. We are more accepting of each other as we know each other so well. I've watched other relationships fall apart and it scared me, making me doubt our relationship would last. It is amazing to look back and see how big a part love and commitment played in our relationship. Relationships need both in order to flourish. It is the same way in ministry—love and perseverance are both necessary to thrive.

I came across this verse and thought, "What a wonderful prayer for what people need in the midst of ministry!": "May the Lord direct your hearts into God's love and Christ's perseverance." The Thessalonians had experienced persecution and suffering; they were hearing false teaching and hadn't seen their mentor, Paul, for a while. He had tried to visit them but was unable to do so. While the Thessalonians were doing well overall—they were growing and faithful—they needed encouragement and sound teaching.

It struck me that, as the Thessalonians faced difficult circumstances, Paul prayed that the Lord would direct their hearts into these two areas: the love of God and the perseverance of Christ.

In looking at the challenges we face in cross-cultural ministry, I would think that these two things would be foundational to our lives and ministry. If our hearts were directed into God's love and Christ's perseverance, our lives and ministry would be abundantly fruitful and God would be honored!

So what I would like to do is explore these two areas and to pray, as Paul did for the Thessalonians, that God will direct our hearts into God's love and Christ's perseverance.

God's love . . . we all know he loves us. Everyone reading this has probably memorized John 3:16: "For God so loved the world that he gave his one and only Son, that whoever believes in him shall not perish but have eternal life." Even unbelievers in our home countries have probably heard that God loves them or God is love. However, when we truly know and experience the love of God, it encourages us to persevere. Knowing his love gives us security in the midst of trials and also influences our relationships with others.

Read Romans 8:31–39:

> What, then, shall we say in response to these things? If
> God is for us, who can be against us? He who did not
> spare his own Son, but gave him up for us all—how
> will he not also, along with him, graciously give us all
> things? Who will bring any charge against those whom
> God has chosen? It is God who justifies. Who then
> is the one who condemns? No one. Christ Jesus who
> died—more than that, who was raised to life—is at the
> right hand of God and is also interceding for us. Who
> shall separate us from the love of Christ? Shall trouble
> or hardship or persecution or famine or nakedness or
> danger or sword? As it is written:
>
> "For your sake we face death all day long; we are consid-
> ered as sheep to be slaughtered."
>
> No, in all these things we are more than conquerors
> through him who loved us. For I am convinced that
> neither death nor life, neither angels nor demons, neither

the present nor the future, nor any powers, neither height
nor depth, nor anything else in all creation, will be able
to separate us from the love of God that is in Christ Jesus
our Lord.

God's love for us is so great that he was willing to give up his
own Son. Why do we think he will withhold anything from us after
having done that? Nothing is able to separate us from the love of
God. Facing difficulties doesn't mean we are further from God's
love. Paul recognizes this when he lists things that are scary or
drastic—like facing death all day long—as things that we would
be tempted to think would be powerful enough to affect us. But he
lists these things to show that none of them is powerful enough to
separate us or keep us from God's love. Absolutely nothing can come
between us and his love for us.

Now I know you know this. If someone were to ask you, "Does
God love you?" you would answer, "Yes!" But I want us to think
about it for a few minutes and ask ourselves a few questions. Would
God love me as much even if I wasn't trying to be obedient and
good? Would he love me as much if I wasn't a cross-cultural worker?

About eight years into our ministry we were home on leave and
I got sick. We were supposed to be home for six months, and when
I got sick we had to stay longer. We ended up staying in our home
country about a year. During that year we weren't even certain we
could go back because, though doctors were running different tests,
they were having a hard time figuring out what was wrong with me.

I felt guilty. It was my fault we weren't back overseas. I felt sick,
partly because I was. But beyond that, I also felt heartsick. I felt
lost. What if we couldn't return overseas? What would we do? Who
would I be?

I began to realize how closely I associated my worth and identity
with what I did. Who I was as a person—what made me valuable in
my own eyes—was intricately tied up with my actions.

I was also a little worried about our marriage. I read that 75
percent of marriages with a chronically ill spouse ended in divorce.

When I told my husband that statistic, he simply said, "Well, let's be among that 25 percent." I appreciated his commitment, but felt the heavy responsibility that I might change the course of our careers. I also wondered how other people would view me if I wasn't a cross-cultural worker. I didn't look sick. My illness was not visible. It wasn't like having a cast or wheelchair that would immediately communicate to others that I was ill. Would I be seen as a quitter? Would I lose their respect? Who would I be without that identity? And then . . . how does God view me? Is this illness from him as a form of discipline? What did I do wrong to bring this on? Was he angry with me? What could I do to get him to make me well again?

I didn't think much about the love of God in those days. I didn't feel all that loved. I felt scared of God and what he was going to do. I was afraid of his will for me, which was a big clue that I wasn't 100 percent convinced of his love for me.

It's true, isn't it? It's hard to feel loved when we are hurting. It's also hard to recognize God's love when we somehow think it is dependent on what we do.

My friend Robynn shared her view of God's love in our book *Expectations and Burnout: Women Surviving the Great Commission.* She wrote about how it changed through her experience with burnout and consequent counseling:

> First of all, I began to grasp that God really does love
> me. He notices me. He sees me. This is the type of lesson
> you learn in Sunday school. This is the prerequisite to
> growth in Christ, yet somehow I'd skipped it. I didn't
> connect with that love. I had preached it to others but I
> didn't believe it to be true of me. I didn't realize how he's
> not really that impressed with what I do, especially the
> stuff He hasn't asked me to do . . . but he is impressed
> with me! He treasures me! He loves me! He created me
> and of all creation I am his prized possession (Isaiah 43:1;
> 62:5, James 1:18). If I believed, and I did, that God's love
> for me was tenuous and fragile, then it made sense that
> I'd work unrealistically hard to be lovable and to win

his favor. I wish I would have known that God loves me,
and it doesn't matter what I do or where I live, that love
doesn't change. Knowing God's love for me, knowing
that He treasures me, would have made His sovereignty
less maddening, I think. I wish I would have known that.
(Eenigenburg and Bliss 2010: 218–19)

It doesn't matter what we do, where we go, what we've done or
will face. God loves us with an everlasting love, and there is nothing
on earth or in the heavens that can separate us from that love.
Everything has limits . . . except God's love.

How does this unconditional love work? We may experience
it from our parents and grandparents to a certain degree. I know I
always felt loved by family. However, in schools we are "loved" (or
maybe "valued" is a better word) when we obey our teachers, get
good grades, and stay out of trouble. The love or value we receive
and perceive from others is mostly dependent on how we act or what
we do.

Robert McGee, author of the book *The Search for Significance*,
says most people believe these three things:

1. I must meet certain standards to feel good about myself.
2. I must be approved by certain others to feel good about myself.
3. Those who fail are unworthy of love and deserve to be punished.

The equation he uses to summarize this in his book is this:

Self-worth = Performance + Others' opinions.
(2003, p. 42)

The entire book looks at the basis of our significance in God's
eyes, and the truth is that our significance has nothing to do with
what we do or what others think about us. Our performance and
others' opinions of us have no effect on our value as people. God
loves us simply because he does, whether we are good or bad,
succeed or fail, serve across cultures or serve customers at a restaurant in our hometown.

God's love isn't dependent on what we do. He loved us when he knew how bad we were, while we were still sinners. When we were his enemies, Christ died for us. He died knowing that there would be those who rejected his sacrifice, and yet he still loved the world. When we mess up, when we sin or do something ungodly, it doesn't change God's love for us. It may change our circumstances; we may face results or consequences. But we are always loved. His love is not based on us, but on who he is. Because of this, his love is unchanging, fathomless, and eternal.

Some of our unbelieving friends are fearful that we could live however we want since God's unconditional love isn't dependent on our actions. That kind of grace and love is too scary, too freeing. I would counter that when we are loved like that, yes, it is freeing. However, it isn't the freedom to sin and live how we want apart from God, because we recognize the cost of our forgiveness. It is the freedom to live for him as we dedicate ourselves to following hard after him. We are free to face good and bad, easy and hard, knowing we are cared for and loved by Almighty God.

So, knowing we are totally and thoroughly loved with an unchanging, eternal love not only gives us security and endurance as we persevere in the face of difficulties, it also affects, or should affect, our relationships. This love that we experience from God should flow through us into our interactions with others.

Paul prays for the Ephesians in chapter 3:14–21:

> For this reason I kneel before the Father, from whom
> every family in heaven and on earth derives its name.
> I pray that out of his glorious riches he may strengthen
> you with power through his Spirit in your inner being,
> so that Christ may dwell in your hearts through faith.
> And I pray that you, being rooted and established in
> love, may have power, together with all the Lord's holy
> people, to grasp how wide and long and high and deep is
> the love of Christ, and to know this love that surpasses

knowledge—that you may be filled to the measure of all
the fullness of God.

Now to him who is able to do immeasurably more than
all we ask or imagine, according to his power that is at
work within us, to him be glory in the church and in
Christ Jesus throughout all generations, forever and ever!

Amen.

Paul prays that they would be rooted and established in love
so that *together with the saints* they would know how wide, long,
high, and deep the love of Christ is. This love is something that we
not only experience as individual children of God, but as the body
of Christ. It is this love that makes us stand out as his disciples.
Whether we love our families, friends, brothers and sisters in Christ,
coworkers, enemies, or those coworkers we view as enemies, it is his
love that makes it possible. Paul prays that the Ephesians would comprehend this love together with the saints—as the body of Christ.

Anyone who has been involved in cross-cultural ministry longer
than two days knows that loving our teammates is often our biggest
challenge. Whether they don't meet our expectations, offend us by
things they say or do, or have a difference of opinion as to how to do
things, or even if there is just a personality clash, there are almost
always relationship challenges. Sometimes we aren't as loving
toward each other as we should be, and when we do not love each
other we are tarnishing our witness for Christ and shaming the very
name we long to honor.

Teams that are living out this love have a stronger testimony in
the community than those who are holding grudges and withholding
forgiveness. Who would be impressed with the power and person of
Christ if he cannot make a difference in how we treat those that we
are supposed to love?

I can think of two ways to address this lack of love for each other.
One, we need to revel in the love God has for us. The security and
freedom that his love gives us—to know that we are loved no matter

what happens or what we do—compels us to live without fear that we will mess up that relationship. He knows everything about us and still loves us. We must meditate on the love that God has for us and thank him for it daily. As we do this we will surely notice a definitive difference in how we love others. When I know I am loved and am secure in that love, it is much harder to offend me, because my value isn't dependent on what you think of me or say to me. God's love works in us and through us, making us vessels of that love.

Secondly, if we are having a hard time loving our teammates, we need to aggressively work to obey Scripture. Jesus, our Lord, tells us to love one another, and he also tells us to love our enemies. There is no one we are not to love. Matthew 5:44,45 says, "Love your enemies and pray for those who persecute you, that you may be children of your Father in heaven. He causes his sun to rise on the evil and the good, and sends rain on the righteous and the unrighteous." For some reason it seems we often have an easier time applying this with the people with whom we share the good news. But, especially when team relationships are strained, we need to be praying for each other and modeling the love that we have from God, who loves and provides for the good and the wicked.

There have been times when I have asked this question: if a book were written on team harmony, would you look for it among fiction or nonfiction books? Team harmony can be elusive; personalities can be harsh and rigid. Jill Briscoe writes about difficult people in her book *Faith Enough to Finish* (2001: 117):

> I thank God for the difficult people in my life, for I have discovered that they are not always difficult. Many times as I have gotten to know them, they have proved to be different and not difficult. I thank God for their grace in putting up with me!

Too often teams disband before they get to the part where they discover that team members aren't difficult, they are different. Oh that we would have compassion, mercy, and forgiveness for colaborers that speaks volumes in a compassionless, merciless, and bitter world!

Jesus is honored when unconditional love is shown. When we allow bitterness to grow and anger to divide us, he is dishonored and portrayed as less powerful and less important than our own grievances and preferences.

In an informal survey, I asked the women in our organization what builds team harmony. They had some great insights and mentioned some things to do and some attitudes to have.

They encourage team members to recognize that everyone on the team is different and needs to work using their gifts. Commitment to each other shows up in spending time, working, worshiping, praying, and playing with each other. One woman wisely suggested that teams ask their prayer partners to regularly pray intentionally and specifically for team unity. Teams can be proactive in doing team-building events, activities, and training.

Also, we can practice good conflict management by giving others on our team permission to confront us in love when a conflict arises. This permission that has already been given makes it easier for the giver and the receiver of the confrontation. Though it is important to have effective communication, it is vital to expect miscommunication and to seek to clarify what teammates are saying or doing before jumping to conclusions.

One woman told the story of saying something in a team meeting and, in response, one of her teammates gave her a horrible look. Her first thought was, "I can't believe they thought my idea was that bad that they snubbed me like that!" It bothered her the rest of the day. Later that night she finally worked up the courage to ask her teammate why she had made that face. With a smile on her face, her teammate said, "I had a bug land on my lip."

Teammates help each other out. They can celebrate holidays together. They should share a common purpose and understanding of team. They work through difficulties rather than ignoring them, and team becomes a safe place to be.

Character qualities such as trust, openness, humility, vulnerability, honesty, love, integrity, and forgiveness are essential. Expecting the best and giving our teammates the benefit of the doubt are helpful in building team relationships. Teammates should show concern for each other and accept people the way they are and the way they are gifted. Each person's contributions should be valued. When expectations are not met and when conflicts arise, teams need to let forgiveness and mercy flow out of the love they have experienced from God himself.

It is my prayer that God would direct our hearts into his love. Without it, we will not be able to persevere. We will not want to persevere. May you experience his love anew, and may that love influence your relationship with the Lord as well as with friends, family, and teammates for his glory.

Questions:

How does this truth of being loved make a difference in how you live your life and how you relate to others?

How involved should sending churches be when the cross-cultural workers they support are involved in a serious team conflict?

Resource:

Ken Sande, *The Peacemaker: A Biblical Guide to Resolving Personal Conflict*, rev. ed. (Grand Rapids: Baker Books, 2004).

Perseverance

When Don and I began dating, I *really* enjoyed being with him. So whenever he asked me to go jogging, I did. Not because I like to jog. I hate to jog. But I did it because I would be with him. On our honeymoon we got up one morning and he said, "Let's go jogging." I said "Okay" and we went outside. We ran a little bit and I saw a big rock. I said I would wait there for him while he went jogging. He looked a bit baffled; that was the end of our jogging together. When we told our kids about this, they asked their dad if he felt deceived. I hadn't thought of it that way. I didn't mean to deceive him. I never said I liked jogging. I just said I liked him. To be with him I had to jog, so I did! After we were married I could enjoy being with him without jogging.

To me, jogging is boring, hard, tiring, and sweaty. To do it a person needs perseverance. Perseverance has been defined as a "steady persistence in a course of action or purpose, especially in spite of difficulties, obstacles or discouragement" (http://www.dictionary.com). Persevering is hard work. It was easy to persevere during the vacation we took in Hawaii. There weren't many obstacles, difficulties, or discouragement! I could have even persevered in that tropical paradise longer than the one week we spent there!

However, in cross-cultural ministry, persevering is far from easy. There are plenty of obstacles. Discouragements abound. Difficulties arise almost daily.

Our theme verse for this section is found in 2 Thessalonians 3:5: "May the Lord direct your hearts into God's love and Christ's perseverance." In the previous chapter we looked at the love of God and how it gives us security and influences our relationships with others. Now let's take a look at the perseverance of Christ, beginning by reading Hebrews 12:1–3:

Therefore, since we have so a great cloud of witnesses
surrounding us, let us also lay aside every encumbrance
and the sin which so easily entangles us, and let us run
with endurance the race that is set before us, fixing our
eyes on Jesus, the author and perfecter of faith, who for
the joy set before Him endured the cross, despising the
shame, and has sat down at the right hand of the throne
of God.

For consider Him who has endured such hostility by
sinners against Himself, so that you will not grow weary
and lose heart. (NASB)

The previous chapter in Hebrews is filled with examples of people
who persevered through trials by walking by faith. None of those mentioned were perfect, saint-like people. They all had their problems and
sin issues, but they all had faith in God. Some had really great endings
to their stories. Walls fell down, people were healed, and enemies
were defeated. Others didn't seem to have very happy endings. They
were flogged, killed, and left destitute. Of course, every one of them
had ultimate happy endings because God took them home to heaven.
Whatever the outcome here on earth, they had faith in God and persevered through the good and the bad because they trusted that the best
was, as yet, unseen and still to come.

Hebrews chapter 12 tells us we are surrounded by a great cloud
of witnesses, those who have gone before us persevering by faith.
They are all with God now and have no need for faith. They are
walking by sight. Today, while we are alive here on this planet, is the
only opportunity we have to walk by faith. One day we will see him
and walk by sight. Until then we are to walk by faith, persevering in
our race, keeping our eyes on Jesus.

The writer tells us to throw off anything that hinders us, any
sin that entangles us, so that we can run our race with perseverance.
I think running is hard even when a person is dressed for it! I can
only imagine how much harder it is being weighed down by carrying
anything heavy.

Most of us, in order to be accepted by our agencies and sent out by our churches, have been examined and found "good enough" (for lack of a better term) to become cross-cultural workers. Normally we're not murderers, though we may be more tempted in this area as we face challenges overseas! We aren't hardened criminals, habitual thieves, or chronic liars. However, let's not fool ourselves. We are still depraved sinners and need to be careful of sins that can easily beset us and weigh us down.

I believe that we can be more susceptible to temptation in a cross-cultural environment. We are away from our normal support systems and comfort zones. It is easy to become lonely, to miss hearing our own language and fitting in. We can begin to rationalize bad choices. During our first year overseas I longed to hear English and began watching anything that I could find in English on TV. There wasn't much available, but I became intrigued with an American soap opera. I would have never watched it in the States, but when living overseas it seemed it should be alright to watch— after all it was in English and I needed to hear some English! On the soap opera, all the characters' lives were so messed up because of immoral relationships and poor choices. Night after night I watched as sin was demonstrated as the norm for their lives. It must have weighed heavily on my heart because one day I actually found myself praying for the characters on the show! God reminded me that these people were not real. I knew I had to stop watching and start practicing self-control and pursuing holiness.

We must be alert, knowing ourselves and our weaknesses. I'm sure we've heard of those involved in ministry who would have been highly unlikely to become sexually involved before or outside of marriage in their home countries, but stumbled in these areas on the field. Once overseas it appears to be easier to fall away from our convictions. The loneliness can be overwhelming.

When we first arrived in South Asia, I knew three people. I didn't know where to go, and even if I could go somewhere, I didn't know how to get back to where I was living. It was confusing;

I wanted to meet people, but it was so hard. I missed friends from home and was tempted to spend too much time on the computer chatting with them.

I think the loneliness that we feel when working across cultures can cause us to be more susceptible to pursuing risky relationships. I've read that Internet pornography is a huge problem for male pastors and those serving across cultures; however, it is on the rise as a problem for women as well. Some marriages fall apart due to spouses connecting with old friends of the opposite sex on Facebook and pursuing those relationships. Let's be on our guard, even in the midst of our loneliness. We need to know where we are most easily tempted so that we can be on the lookout, get rid of these sins, and run the race we have in front of us.

It isn't just how we run, but what we are looking at as we run. We are to look to Jesus, the author and perfecter of our faith. The Greek word for "author" contains the idea of Jesus being the pioneer or leader of our faith. He is also the perfecter of our faith. He completes it; he perfects it. To persevere in order to finish our race, we are to fix our eyes on him who knows what it is to persevere. He endured the Cross, finished what God called him to do, and sat down at God's right hand. He looked beyond what he was enduring and ahead to the joy set before him. We, too, need to keep our eyes focused beyond what we are dealing with today, fixing them on him who is eternal. In any race, the runner is looking to the end, the goal. We must have an eternal perspective, one that keeps Jesus Christ in the forefront of our decisions, actions, and attitudes.

Wearing bracelets with WWJD (What would Jesus do?) on them was a fad a few years back. My daughter was thinking of buying one and then asked herself what Jesus would do. She decided not to buy one based on the answer to that very question! The concept of asking ourselves that question, though somewhat trite and overused now, is not a bad idea. Imagine asking that before watching a questionable movie, reading an unhealthy book, or pursuing an improper relationship on Facebook. What would Jesus do?

We are not only to look to Jesus, but to consider him. Jesus endured opposition from sinful people. No matter what we've faced, we have not endured what Jesus did. Because he is our example, our leader and, indeed, our focus, there is no reason for us to grow so weary that we lose heart.

When do we feel the weariest? When is it easiest to lose heart? It is when we lose sight of the big picture and get caught up in our present difficulties. When we take our eyes off of Jesus, we focus on what we are facing. Jesus becomes smaller and our problems become bigger. I find it easier to endure loneliness or cultural confusion or crowded, big cities when I know it serves a bigger purpose. If I lose sight of that big picture—the kingdom of God and the glory of Jesus—all I can see is my own dilemma. Everything and everyone else grows dim, and I become the center of my own little universe. When I am my focus, trials and troubles become my enemies. They make me uncomfortable, and so I dislike them. I grow weary and lose heart because I feel I must take charge, because my own happiness—which becomes all important—is at stake.

When I look at Jesus, when he is my focus, it is easier to see trials and troubles as opportunities to trust him, because I'm thinking of him being in charge of the bigger picture. Looking to Jesus gives us heart and encourages us to persevere and not grow weary. He reminds us that he has a grand plan, and we are a part of it *for him.* It isn't all about me and what I am going through. Instead, it's about thinking long term and being committed to his will no matter what and to how he will work through our difficulties for his rightful glory.

Hebrews 12:4–13 gives us another perspective on enduring hardship:

> In your struggle against sin, you have not yet resisted to the point of shedding your blood. And have you completely forgotten this word of encouragement that addresses you as a father addresses his son? It says,
>
> "My son, do not make light of the Lord's discipline, and do not lose heart when he rebukes you, because the Lord

disciplines the one he loves, and he chastens everyone he accepts as his son."

Endure hardship as discipline; God is treating you as his children. For what children are not disciplined by their father? If you are not disciplined—and everyone undergoes discipline—then you are not legitimate, not true sons and daughters at all. Moreover, we have all had human fathers who disciplined us and we respected them for it. How much more should we submit to the Father of spirits and live! They disciplined us for a little while as they thought best; but God disciplines us for our good, in order that we may share in his holiness. No discipline seems pleasant at the time, but painful. Later on, however, it produces a harvest of righteousness and peace for those who have been trained by it.

Therefore, strengthen your feeble arms and weak knees. "Make level paths for your feet," so that the lame may not be disabled, but rather healed.

The writer of Hebrews reminds readers of what is written in Proverbs 3:11,12 about the discipline of the Lord for those he loves. As our Father, God sometimes gives us opportunities to endure hardship simply because we are his children and he loves us. He disciplines us in all his wisdom for our good. We, as parents, discipline our own children even with our limited perspective. Disciplining my children as they were growing up was difficult. I felt inadequate many times. There were times I was so tired I wanted to pretend I didn't see the disobedience, but I knew I had to be proactive. Though I know I failed at times, I also know that I worked hard to discipline them consistently and lovingly. Today I am thankful for the time we invested in doing so. Our children know they were loved, and they are so gracious to have forgiven us for our shortcomings. We thank God we all survived their childhood years!

No one likes being disciplined. It hurts! But, later on, it is worth it because of what it produces in those who have been trained by it.

There have been times when I've been in the midst of a difficulty and I took a minute to think, "Wow. This is hard, but God is disciplining me, and this means he loves me. I am his child. This is going to be good for me." It's kind of like going to the dentist. I hate going to the dentist, but I go because I know that in the end it will be good for me. It's better for me in the long run to endure a little pain now rather than a lot of pain later on.

Knowing that I am loved by God enough that he disciplines me, and being confident that he knows what is best, is comforting. I think one of the hardest things about being a parent is wanting to do what is best for your child and sometimes not knowing what the best is.

I remember when our oldest son was around four years old, he found a cricket in our house and proceeded to spend the morning playing with it. He would pick it up, try to put it in his little matchbox cars, watch it try to get away, and catch it again. They were having a great time playing . . . well at least Stephen was. I'm not too sure about the cricket.

It was almost time for lunch, and then it would be nap time for him and me. I thought I should try to prepare him to let the cricket go. I was thinking he would be sad or angry because he wouldn't want to. So I started earlier than necessary and began by gently saying, "Stephen, it's about time for your nap. I think the cricket is almost ready to go outside and play. Maybe he wants a nap. Soon we need to let him go." Stephen stopped, looked at me, and said, "I can't play with the cricket anymore?" I was getting ready for tears, ready for him to beg me to let him play with the cricket a little longer. Instead he calmly put the cricket on the floor, stepped on it, and walked away. Hmm. That wasn't so hard.

Then there were other times I thought something would be easy and didn't take the time to prepare the children for what was ahead. When I was exchanging summer clothes for winter ones, one daughter was upset to the point of tears. I hadn't even thought about it potentially being traumatic! I learned that she needed more warning of any changes that were to come. I began a few months ahead saying, "You know, pretty soon the weather will change and we'll need to get heavier clothes out." That seemed to help.

Looking back, there were fights to arbitrate and quarrels to settle without knowing how they were started or who was at fault. It didn't help that the witnesses were always biased and all had different stories of who started what and how! Long road trips with statements like "she touched me" or "he looked at me" seemed even longer as we divided our time between driving, navigating, and refereeing fights!

We do our best, but it isn't easy. God, however, *always* knows and does what is best. He *always* knows what I need. He *always* knows the outcome and how I will respond. The Creator God, my heavenly Father *always* has my best interests in mind! He is a perfect Father, and knowing he is at work in me can change my perspective of what I am facing in amazing ways. I can fully trust him. *Always.*

However, enduring hardship and recognizing that sometimes it is discipline, and is therefore good for me, doesn't just affect me. It also influences others. Look at verses 12,13: we strengthen our arms and knees, and make level paths so that the lame may not be disabled, but rather healed. Our strength, which we gain and which grows stronger through enduring hardship, will benefit others.

I think it is interesting to note how intertwined our lives are as believers. John Donne was right when he wrote that no man is an island. Do you remember Joshua 7, when Achan sinned by taking what he was told not to take from the plunder? He was not the only one who suffered for his sin; thirty-six Israelites were killed in the lost battle against Ai. Also, his sons and daughters and animals were put to death. Joshua 22:20 says, "When Achan son of Zerah was unfaithful in regard to the devoted things, did not wrath come on the whole community of Israel? He was not the only one who died for his sin." When we sin, we never just hurt ourselves. Others are always influenced by the evil we commit, and we are of limited use to God when we are sinning.

I remember being greatly challenged by a pastor that I really admired. I was amazed how God was using him. When I first found out that he had been unfaithful to his wife, I was saddened and initially felt that all the words he spoke that had ministered to me so effectively lost most of their meaning. It hurt not only me, but many members of that local fellowship. We all suffered consequences from one person's sin.

On the other hand, when we do what is good, we influence others as well. An obvious example of this in Scripture is Ruth who, through her endurance in doing good, was not only a blessing to Naomi, but to Boaz, the nation of Israel and, ultimately, to us as she is in the lineage of our Savior. There are many other scriptural examples of people doing good and affecting others. We just have to read of individuals like Nehemiah, Daniel, Joseph, the Israelite midwives in Egypt, and Mary to see how their actions affected so many others for God's glory.

There are also those who have influenced us in our lifetimes. I can think of many people who have invested in me, and I have had many role models—people I've looked to who have endured hardship and by their example and words have encouraged me to do the same. There were youth leaders who took the time to answer my many questions and who gave me opportunity to serve in the church and use my spiritual gifts. Women who have listened to my concerns and prayed for me have kept me from despairing when despair looked like my only option. To this day I thank God for that group of moms who met together every week to pray for each other. I could share my heart there and know that nothing said would ever leave that room. We could cry and share our heavy loads. Advice wasn't sought, nor was it often given. The only responses were lots of unconditional love and powerful praying. They were a lifeline for me during a difficult time.

When we endure hardship, keeping our eyes on Jesus, we will be strengthened. When we accept discipline from the hand of God who loves us and learn from him, we will be strengthened. As we are strengthened we are able to endure and do good; we can then come alongside and help others who may be feeling weak so that they, too, can endure for the glory of God.

Love and perseverance are either quite evident or glaringly missing when suffering comes. A woman cannot be a mother or a cross-cultural worker without expecting some suffering. God communicates to us through Scripture, empowering us so that we don't merely endure through suffering, but rejoice as we persevere through it.

Questions:

What has been causing your soul to grow weary as you face temptations living in a different culture, and how have you responded to it?

Why do cross-cultural workers grow so weary? How can home churches be a help to them?

Resource:

Richard A. Swenson, *Margin: Restoring Emotional, Physical, Financial, and Time Reserves to Overloaded Lives* (Colorado Springs: NavPress, 2004).

Rejoice in Suffering

When Robynn and I were waiting to hear from the publisher to see if they were going to publish our book exploring expectations and burnout among women in cross-cultural ministry, I wondered about halfway through if it was possible to experience burnout while writing a book about burnout! Writing it, having it edited, rewriting it, working through it and making more changes, wondering if it would even be published after all of the hard work, falling behind in other areas of responsibility . . . I was feeling very stressed and tired. Now, after finishing it by God's grace, I look back with a strong sense of accomplishment. It feels good to have seen a difficult project through to the end. I learned a lot through the process. I feel like my character has been developed more, I know more about endurance because I didn't give up. My friend Robynn, who cowrote it with me, had experienced burnout, endured many physical side effects, dealt with sorrows, thefts, persecution and suffering, her own and that of close friends. Through the course of healing, she has grown in her understanding of herself, others, and God. She reports that she is glad she is not the same person she was before all of these sufferings. Scripture tells us that we can rejoice in our sufferings because we know that suffering can have good results. Just read Romans 5:1–11:

> Therefore, since we have been justified through faith,
> we have peace with God through our Lord Jesus Christ,
> through whom we have gained access by faith into this
> grace in which we now stand. And we boast in the hope
> of the glory of God. Not only so, but we also glory in
> our sufferings, because we know that suffering produces
> perseverance; perseverance, character; and character,
> hope. And hope does not put us to shame, because God's

love has been poured out into our hearts through the Holy
Spirit, who has been given us.

You see, at just the right time, when we were still power-
less, Christ died for the ungodly. Very rarely will anyone
die for a righteous person, though for a good person
someone might possibly dare to die. But God demon-
strates his own love for us in this: While we were still
sinners, Christ died for us.

Since we have now been justified by his blood, how much
more shall we be saved from God's wrath through him!
For if, while we were God's enemies, we were reconciled
to him through the death of his Son, how much more,
having been reconciled, shall we be saved through his
life! Not only is this so, but we also boast in God through
our Lord Jesus Christ, through whom we have now received reconciliation.

Jesus paved the way for us to stand in God's grace. We have
been justified through faith, and because of Jesus Christ we have
peace with God. Because of this relationship with God, we can
rejoice in the hope we have of bringing glory to God through our
trials. One of the reasons that Robynn and I worked on our book—
one of the driving forces behind wanting to finish it—was that we
hoped to glorify God through it. Nothing thrills my heart like thinking that something I do or think or say can actually bring glory to
God. Not only can we rejoice in that, but we can also rejoice in our
sufferings, because we know that suffering produces good fruit in
our lives that will ultimately also bring glory to God.

In many of the countries where we work, being a believer in
Jesus is not easy. There are those who have lost their homes, jobs,
and even their lives because of their faith. It's also not easy being a
cross-cultural worker. We can face suffering, betrayal, and persecution. Husbands coming home from a trip are turned away at the
border, and their wives are left to pack up the house and move the
family to join him in a different country. One of my friends was held

in detention when she returned from a trip and tried to enter her host country. After several days she was eventually forced to leave her husband and four sons behind until they could join her in a different country. Here is Lori's story:

June 30, 2002 (sometime after 10:30 a.m.)

I am sitting in an area reserved for undesirables in the airport. Right now I am waiting for an interview with the officer in charge. I am very hungry and am glad I had a big piece of pizza before I got on the plane last night. When I arrived at 9:30 p.m. on June 29, I needed to get an entry visa. I went to a bank window, but the teller sent me to another, explaining that I needed dollars to buy a visa. When I got to the window of the second bank, the teller closed the window. I then proceeded to try the third bank. He was willing to take local currency and give me change in dollars. So, I finally had my $15 visa. I proceeded to passport/visa control.

After I stood in line for a while, a man stamped the visa in my passport and passed it on to the computer person behind him. I then picked up my luggage. Because I had gone to another country to pick up mail, I had a large suitcase full of letters. I was praying about the suitcase—that it would not be opened—when I took my place in the "nothing to declare" line. Then, out of the blue, the man that had stamped my passport came running up to me and said that I needed to come with him. I'm glad I had my carry-on with wheels so that I could pull it easily. I followed the man away from the hustle and bustle of airline passengers into an area with mostly white-uniformed airport security guards. They asked me to put my luggage down in a hallway and then take a seat until called.

I remember walking into the narrow hallway with orange bus terminal-like chairs where I saw about nine people from different countries—Nigeria, Senegal, Kenya, and Somalia. Very surprised to see a westerner join them, they told me they had been there for three days and had not yet gotten to make a telephone call. I was aghast at this infringement of their rights. I wrote all their contact numbers on the throw-up bag I was going to give the kids, assuming that I would get out soon and be able to help them by communicating with their families. They asked if all my papers were in order and I told them they were. I explained that I thought I was being detained because of telling people about Jesus.

A guard soon called me into an office with three plain-clothed policemen. One of them questioned me regarding what my job was, who my husband was, what he did and if he had ever been in trouble. When I asked the policeman why I was being detained, he said he didn't know, but that something had come up on the computer and he was checking it out. After this short interview, I was asked to sit in a nearby lounge away from the other detainees.

After three hours I was informed by a kind guard that I would not be entering my host country. I cried. I cried as if I had just been told someone close to me died. The guard said that I would meet with an officer tomorrow and that maybe he would allow me to enter. A woman guard tried to comfort me. I asked the officer what I would do for the night—I had heard of airport hotels for detainees. When he explained there was a hotel for $98 a night, I quickly realized that I didn't know where the hotel was, and didn't know how I would get back to keep my appointment. I also thought it was a lot of money, and I wasn't too thrilled about being alone with a bunch of men, with no recourse if they did anything inappropriate. The woman guard interrupted my thoughts, "You don't want to go there! I will give you clean sheets and you will be fine here. It is God's will. Don't cry!"

I took her advice and found a bunk in the room for
ladies. Although I had been told I could leave my bags
at their desks, I wasn't comfortable leaving the suitcase
filled with mail out of concern someone would look
through it. I took it with me and slept with it on my bunk.
Exhausted, but unable to sleep, I found comfort in the
scriptures, particularly Philippians 4:6–9. I was at peace
and was not fearful. There were two Nigerian ladies who
had been detained with me. One was my mother's age
and had great faith. We sang some praise songs together
and noted that Paul probably had just as many roaches
in his prison—and even rats, which we hadn't seen. We
had to use the men's bathroom so we helped each other
by going in at the same time. I was comforted by these
ladies and very thankful.

Our room was the only one that was enclosed, so we
had some privacy. During the first night, four different
female airport employees came into the room to pray.
Although we had left the lights on initially to keep the
roaches off of us, the lights went on and off all night.
The last lady to come in was the kind woman guard that
had helped me earlier. She prayed and then sat on my
bed to talk to me when she saw that I was awake. After
she asked me the same questions the secret police had
asked, we began to talk of our faiths. She was seeking
God, but in her darkness she was blind. I praise God
because he gave me words to say and a boldness to say
them. I reasoned that if she was the reason I was not
allowed into this country, then that was okay. I remembered Colossians 3:17, "Whatever you do in word
or deed, do all in the name of the Lord Jesus, giving
thanks to God the Father through Him."

Throughout that first night I asked repeatedly to use the
phone, but was never permitted to make a call. I was very
concerned about Paul and the boys. I was worried that
they would be arrested or something. I know this wasn't

very logical, but at the same time I had to trust the Lord, believing that he would take care of them.

After 12:00 p.m.

Well, I just finished with my interview with the officer. He made it clear that I am not going into my host country. He said that the embassy had contacted them and they had communicated to them the reason for my detainment. I asked him what that reason was. He pointed his finger at me and said, "You know the reason." I told him that I couldn't think of anything except that I tell anyone I can about Jesus. He asked, "What do you tell them?" I told him that I tell people that Jesus died on the cross and rose again on the third day and that without a relationship with him we will not have eternal life. He asked, "Isn't that what the New Testament says?" I replied that yes, what I shared with people were truths from the Bible. He told me that someone had complained about me. I couldn't think of anyone that would do this to me. I went through my list of contacts and evaluated if I had said anything that would have inflamed them against me. I couldn't think of any of them who would complain. I asked if they had detained women in my position before and he said that women could cause as many problems as men! I laughed because, of course, he is right. I asked him if I could call my husband. He said I could. Then I asked him how I could leave. He said I could go anywhere I wanted to go. I just needed a ticket.

After a few hours I was able to call Paul. When I heard his voice, I cried. I tried not to, but I just couldn't help it. He told me that he had been in contact with the embassy and they had said that unofficially I was not allowed into the country because I had shared the gospel. He then said he was on his way to come and see me.

Paul showed up and they escorted me to a door where I met Paul. I cried again. It was so good to see him. We

had about five minutes to talk and he asked me if I was
willing to try entering this country through another
port of entry. I told him I had had enough. The country
didn't want me and I didn't need to be told twice. He
had brought a bag with him to give to me. It held bottled
water, M&Ms, undergarments and two magazines. The
guards then made him leave. He promised me that he
would get me out as soon as he could get me on a flight
to another country. I felt better just seeing him because
I knew he was okay and safe. I returned to the detention
area and feasted on the supper provided which was pita
bread and feta cheese. The Nigerians would not touch
the bread because it smelled like manure. But I was so
hungry I didn't care. They also provided melon, which
was a real treat.

I couldn't help but wish the embassy would just let me
stay long enough to pack and say goodbye. I still had two
months left on my visa and was saddened most because I
couldn't say good-bye.

I had my Bible, journal and a novel. I had enough reading
material. That helped me pass the time. We didn't have
much room to walk around in the detention area. I found
that I needed to stay on my bunk rather than in the main
hallway. Men were coming in and out of the bathroom
half-dressed and the guards would change their clothes
in front of us. It was hard to find a place to look so that I
wasn't grossed out. But again, I thank God that we had
a semi-private area in which to dress and be comfortable. Unfortunately the guards would sometimes open
our door to get to their lockers without knocking. So we
depended on each other to guard the door when we were
dressing. I stayed up late the second night so that I could
say good-bye to the Nigerians who were leaving. It was
sad to see friends leave, while I was still left behind.
There was another woman who still had to wait for two
days before leaving, so I wasn't alone. We shared some

M&Ms and went to bed (with the light on because of the cockroaches). I slept great.

July 1, 2002

I was awakened by the lady guard. She brought me a sandwich and said that my husband was on the way with my ticket. I needed to be ready in half an hour. The sandwich was wonderful and what I couldn't eat I gave to a national man who wasn't allowed to eat. I took a big risk and took a shower. I closed the outside bathroom door and then the stall door. While I was taking a shower a man asked if he could come in. I said no in my meanest voice. I heard only a loud sigh. I was able to leave there clean. At noon they came and took me to get a boarding pass and check my luggage. I followed the guard to the airline counter. He talked to three men before he asked me to talk to the ticket agent, who asked me if I had money to buy another ticket if Cyprus didn't want me. I wanted to cry. I had never felt so unwanted in my life. I told him I had the money. Then he begrudgingly pro-cessed me. The guard allowed me to see Paul through a glass wall. Paul climbed the railing so we could hear each other. Paul asked the guard if I had a boarding pass and then he wrote me a quick note. I touched his hand and cried as I said good-bye. The note said not to be ashamed, to walk with my head held high because I was leaving honorably.

So I straightened up, dried my eyes and walked with my head held high. I was returned to the detention area until my flight was scheduled to leave. Then I was escorted to the boarding line of my flight. The guard held back because he said if the flight attendant saw him, there would be problems. So after I passed through that he escorted me to the plane. My lady guard friend came to hug me and say good-bye. I got on the plane and sat for an hour without air conditioning. We finally took off.

We were just receiving our snacks when the pilot's voice came over the intercom and said we had to turn the plane around and go back because we could not land in Cyprus. What! I just laughed at what the guards would say when they saw me again. I pleaded with God that I would not have to go back. The plane started turning around again and we finally landed in Cyprus.

After landing I began to pray as I stood in line for passport/visa control. I didn't know if they would allow me to enter. But there was no problem at all. I was looking for my ride. I started to get worried that no one would come. Then I remembered that Paul said there would be someone and there was. What a relief! I was free.

My family joined me two weeks later and, though it had been a difficult situation, God brought me to a greater understanding of his grace *through* it.

Lori was honoring the Lord through her suffering and bringing glory to God by seeking to share the gospel with those who hadn't heard it. Workers like her have been jailed, attacked, and killed. Women workers have been sexually harassed and abused, and sadly Majority World believers are usually treated even more harshly. My heart breaks for the families of those imprisoned, tortured, and killed for their faith. I grieve for them . . . and yet, shouldn't we *all* be willing to offer everything, including our lives, for Jesus? All of us know of those who have followed Jesus in this life only to lose much of what this world has to temporarily offer. The cost of discipleship is high, but shouldn't be unexpected. Peter tells us not to be surprised when we suffer. He writes in 1 Peter 4:12–16:

> Dear friends, do not be surprised at the fiery ordeal that has come on you to test you, as though something strange were happening to you. But rejoice inasmuch as you participate in the sufferings of Christ, so that you may be overjoyed when his glory is revealed. If you are insulted because of the name of Christ, you are blessed, for the

Spirit of glory and of God rests on you. If you suffer, it
should not be as a murderer or thief or any other kind of
criminal, or even as a meddler. However, if you suffer as
a Christian, do not be ashamed, but praise God that you
bear that name.

Peter affirms that when we suffer for Jesus, we are blessed and
we know that his glory will be revealed through it. At times we can't
see it, but by faith we wait for his glory to shine. Both Peter and Paul
knew that suffering as believers was to be expected.

Paul says in Romans 5:3–5 that not only can we glorify God in
our sufferings, but we can rejoice in them because we know that they
will ultimately bring about good things in our lives. Suffering brings
about perseverance. Perseverance produces character. Character
results in hope.

Let's briefly take a look at what suffering produces in our lives.
We've already talked a little bit about this: suffering produces perseverance. When we suffer we learn to persevere, to last, to endure
by trusting God. When there is no escape and we must go through
something difficult, we see God's faithfulness and experience his
grace; we learn that we can do it and, by God's grace, we can persevere! When my husband was asked to come in to be questioned by
authorities, our initial reaction was fear. What if he went to jail for
sharing his faith? What would we do? A coworker who had already
been imprisoned for his faith encouraged us not to be afraid; it is
only scary when you haven't experienced it. Once you've been in jail
a few times, it ceases to have a fear factor! He had learned to persevere. Fear tempts us to not persevere, to give up or back down. But it
is as believers persevere, despite being afraid of suffering, that we're
enabled to keep persevering. Dorothy Bernard said, "Courage is fear
that has said its prayers!"

Authorities tried to harass a pastor of a local church in the
Middle East. They wanted him to be afraid. They threatened him
with prison; he said that would give him more time to write and
pray, as well as share his faith with other prisoners. They threatened

to deport him; he said that would give him opportunity to work on some radio sermons he had been asked to preach. They gave up and let him go free. The authorities could not intimidate him, for he had learned to persevere through suffering.

Through suffering we learn to persevere. As we pray and trust God, even when our hearts are frightened, we can persevere by God's grace.

At the time it may feel like we are handling it on our own. Often it is only by looking back that we can see how God helped and empowered us. I don't want to say that it becomes easier, the more things we endure, but we aren't as afraid and we don't feel as alone. We know God was with us in the past and that he gives us hope for the future.

James also talks about perseverance being a benefit of going through trials in chapter 1:2–4: "Consider it pure joy, my brothers and sisters, whenever you face trials of many kinds, because you know that the testing of your faith develops perseverance. Let perseverance finish its work so that you may be mature and complete, not lacking anything." Not only do we learn perseverance, but we see that it also produces maturity in our lives. I think this leads us once again to Romans chapter 5 where Paul talks about perseverance producing character.

How long have you been involved in overseas ministry? No matter how long we've been serving cross-culturally, would you agree that we are not the same people we were when we first left our home countries? Think about who you were and what you were like when you first left to serve overseas. Write down some adjectives that you would use to describe yourself when you first left to serve cross-culturally. Compare that with how you would describe yourself now.

I am deeply grateful that I am not the same person I was when I first left. I didn't think so at the time, but I was somewhat arrogant, self-reliant, ready to take on the world. Today I am more aware of my weaknesses and sins and realize I am more dependent on God.

God has developed character in me through trials, joys, failures, and successes. Persevering has made me a stronger, more whole person. I still have a long way to go in growing and developing spiritually, but I am further along than I was, simply because of persevering through life and ministry.

Character produces hope. We see how God supplies, how he works, how he comes through for us. We learn to trust him even when he doesn't do what we want when we want. We learn more about who he is and who we are, and we develop into people of hope. We see beyond our present difficulties into the future of what God might be doing in and through us and our situations.

In our book *Expectations and Burnout*, Robynn gives an excellent example of how hope evolved in her life journey through her growing understanding of who God is:

> I don't like swimming in the ocean: there are living things lurking beneath the surface; the waves are unpredictable and splash my face; it's cold and deep; there are undertows and pulls that frighten; it's salty and sandy and alive. I do not like swimming in the ocean. I much prefer a swimming pool, a heated pool at that. The temperature is controlled. You can enter at your pleasure, either the deep end or the shallow end. You can go in as far as you like and then climb back out. Blow up a floating device and float on the top if you choose! The bottom is level and smooth. There are no surprises. Nothing lives in a swimming pool.
>
> And that's the kind of God I would prefer as well: one that is controlled and moderate; a God I can measure and understand. I can enter his depths but only as far as I am comfortable. However that's not the kind of God we have. Our God is an ocean of a God. He is alive and dangerous. There are forces at work below his surface. He alone controls the depths, the sprays, the splashes of his personhood. He woos us to the bottom where the water may appear murky and mysterious. Our God is wild and

untamable. He is expansive and unpredictable. When we
say he is holy, we mean he is strange and we do well to
take our shoes off. The ground is holy and the water is
deep. (Eenigenburg and Bliss 2010: 162)

There are some enormous differences between a swimming
pool and an ocean. The pool is tame, measured, and sterile. The
ocean is wild, unpredictable, and filled with living things. How
does this relate to how we hope in God? Can we trust an ocean of a
God? Robynn's point is that through her suffering she has come to
a better understanding of God and recognizes her need to trust him
even when his ways seem wild; as a result of this her hope is made
more sure.

And hope doesn't disappoint us, because God has poured out his
love into our hearts by the Holy Spirit. Again we see a link between
perseverance and love. We know God loves us and we can trust him.

So we see that suffering produces good things—perseverance,
maturity, character, hope, and a growing awareness of the love of
God. We can be confident of God's love because of what he did for
us in Christ. Christ died for us when we were sinners, his enemies.
His love is shown not to be based on who we are or what we do.
His love is founded in who he is. Because of his love, we have been
saved from his wrath and reconciled to him.

Having been reconciled to him, we read in 2 Corinthians 5:17–20
that God has given to us the ministry of reconciliation:

> Therefore, if anyone is in Christ, the new creation has
> come: The old has gone, the new is here! All this is from
> God, who reconciled us to himself through Christ and
> gave us the ministry of reconciliation: that God was
> reconciling the world to himself in Christ, not counting
> people's sins against them. And he has committed to us
> the message of reconciliation. We are therefore Christ's
> ambassadors, as though God were making his appeal
> through us. We implore you on Christ's behalf: Be recon-
> ciled to God.

So not only have we been reconciled to God, we are to seek to help others be reconciled to God as well. This ministry of reconciliation is not easy, and we are called to persevere through suffering to carry it out. We cannot do this on our own. We must rely on the Lord to give grace, strength, and endurance through difficulties. As we do, his message goes forth, he receives glory, and we grow into mature disciples who continue to persevere.

I think Karen Watson had the right perspective. She was a Southern Baptist cross-cultural worker in Iraq who was killed March 15, 2004. She left behind an envelope that said, "Open in case of death." Her letter is quoted in *Lives Given, Not Taken: 21st Century Southern Baptist Martyrs* by Erich Bridges and Jerry Rankin (2005):

> *Dear Pastor Phil and Pastor Roger,*
>
> *You should only be opening this in the event of death. When God calls there are no regrets. I tried to share my heart with you as much as possible, my heart for the nations. I wasn't called to a place; I was called to Him. To obey was my objective, to suffer was expected, His glory my reward . . .*
>
> *The missionary heart:*
>
> ** Cares more than some think is wise*
>
> ** Risks more than some think is safe*
>
> ** Dreams more than some think is practical*
>
> ** Expects more than some think is possible.*
>
> *I was called not to comfort or to success but to obedience . . .*
>
> *There is no Joy outside of knowing Jesus and serving Him. I love you two and my church family.*
>
> *In His care,*
> *Salaam,*
> *Karen*

Questions:
How has persevering changed you since starting your cross-cultural ministry?

How does the church persevere through trials and living countercul-turally in its own country?

Resource:
Charles R. Swindoll, *Three Steps Forward, Two Steps Back: Persevering through Pressure*, rev. ed. (Nashville: Word, 1997).

Endurance and Encouragement from the Word

Being in the Word is essential for perseverance; it is a source of encouragement and endurance. Just read Romans 15:1–7:

> We who are strong ought to bear with the failings of the weak and not to please ourselves. Each of us should please our neighbors for their good, to build them up. For even Christ did not please himself but, as it is written: "The insults of those who insult you have fallen on me." For everything that was written in the past was written to teach us, so that through the endurance taught in the Scriptures and the encouragement they provide we might have hope.
>
> May the God who gives endurance and encouragement give you the same attitude of mind toward each other that Christ Jesus had, so that with one mind and one voice you may glorify the God and Father of our Lord Jesus Christ.
>
> Accept one another, then, just as Christ accepted you, in order to bring praise to God.

After talking about bearing with those who are weak and seeking to build them up just like Jesus did, Paul goes on to say that Scripture was written to teach us, so that through endurance and the encouragement of Scripture we might continually have hope. When we read about Abraham, Jeremiah, Ruth, Esther, Elisha, and others throughout Scripture and how they endured and saw God's faithfulness, we gain encouragement and hope. Since God is the author of his word, he is the ultimate source of this encouragement and ability to endure.

I remember trying to balance my roles as a wife, mother, and cross-cultural worker and feeling stressed in trying to do everything I wanted and/or needed to do. What should my role be? How would God want me to invest my time? I had things to do for my family, for outside the home, for team, for supporters, for myself. Different areas were pulling and vying for my attention. I felt guilty for not putting enough time in any one area and decided to study Scripture to help me determine what my priorities should be. I delved into the lives of women in the Bible, what they did, how they lived, and what happened as a result of their choices and their lives. I began to choose how to invest my time with a clearer understanding and better foundation for making those choices. I had more peace and direction. I could keep going, and it was due to the encouragement and endurance I received from the word of God.

Let me challenge you: if you want to be encouraged and you want to endure, be in the Word regularly. It isn't always easy, but it is always essential. We can't let all the things we see that need to be done—the laundry, cleaning, and cooking—squeeze out what we need to do that we can't see. We also can't let ministry take the place of spending time in the Word. Can we skip days? Sure, it happens. Can we pray while we cook? Yes, we can. However, we have to keep in mind that our souls need nourishment, and merely snacking isn't always the healthiest way to nourish them.

In this same passage we see that God is not only the source of encouragement and endurance; he is also the source for the spirit of unity among those of us who follow Christ, so that together with one heart and mouth we might bring God glory. God delights in the unity of his people. In this passage he is looking at the weak and the strong, the Jews and the Gentiles, and asking us to be like Jesus in accepting one another and seeking to build each other up.

Encouragement and endurance have ripple effects on our relationships, and the result is that God is glorified by all his people.

From Romans 15 we see that to be encouraged and able to endure, we need to be in God's word. The psalmist found this out. Read Psalm 119:81–96 and look for ways he found encouragement and endurance in the Word.

> My soul faints with longing for your salvation,
>> but I have put my hope in your word.
>
> My eyes fail, looking for your promise;
>> I say, "When will you comfort me?"
>
> Though I am like a wineskin in the smoke,
>> I do not forget your decrees.
>
> How long must your servant wait?
>> When will you punish my persecutors?
>
> The arrogant dig pits to trap me,
>> contrary to your law.
>
> All your commands are trustworthy;
>> help me, for I am being persecuted without cause.
>
> They almost wiped me from the earth,
>> but I have not forsaken your precepts.
>
> In your unfailing love preserve my life,
>> that I may obey the statutes of your mouth.
>
> Your word, Lord, is eternal;
>> it stands firm in the heavens.
>
> Your faithfulness continues through all generations;
>> you established the earth, and it endures.
>
> Your laws endure to this day,
>> for all things serve you.
>
> If your law had not been my delight,
>> I would have perished in my affliction.

> I will never forget your precepts,
>   for by them you have preserved my life.
>
> Save me, for I am yours;
>   I have sought out your precepts.
>
> The wicked are waiting to destroy me,
>   but I will ponder your statutes.
>
> To all perfection I see a limit,
>   but your commands are boundless.

I love verses 92,93 especially: "If your law had not been my delight, I would have perished in my affliction. I will never forget your precepts, for by them you have preserved my life." Scripture was at the heart of the psalmist's survival. It will also be at the heart of ours. Those who give up prematurely may have not been spending time in the Word and gaining strength and encouragement from it. Without the Word, we listen to lies and half-truths and start to fall back. Through the Word we are encouraged to persevere.

So far as we've explored perseverance, we've basically looked at it as what we do when we are in the midst of trials. We persevere through them. However, Scripture points out that we are not only to endure as we face difficulties, but we are to actively pursue endurance. Read 1 Timothy 6:9–12, and focus on what he writes about endurance:

> Those who want to get rich fall into temptation and a trap
> and into many foolish and harmful desires that plunge
> people into ruin and destruction. For the love of money is
> a root of all kinds of evil. Some people, eager for money,
> have wandered from the faith and pierced themselves
> with many griefs. But you, man of God, flee from all this,
> and pursue righteousness, godliness, faith, love, endur-
> ance and gentleness. Fight the good fight of the faith.
> Take hold of the eternal life to which you were called
> when you made your good confession in the presence of
> many witnesses.

Paul instructed Timothy to pursue endurance. This word is the same word used elsewhere for perseverance.

Peter tells us to make every effort to persevere in 2 Peter 1:5–11:

> For this very reason, make every effort to add to your
> faith goodness; and to goodness, knowledge; and to
> knowledge, self-control; and to self-control, persever-
> ance; and to perseverance, godliness; and to godliness,
> mutual affection; and to mutual affection, love. For if you
> possess these qualities in increasing measure, they will
> keep you from being ineffective and unproductive in your
> knowledge of our Lord Jesus Christ. But whoever does
> not have them is nearsighted and blind, forgetting that
> they have been cleansed from their past sins.
>
> Therefore, my brothers and sisters, make every effort
> to confirm your calling and election. For if you do these
> things, you will never stumble, and you will receive a
> rich welcome into the eternal kingdom of our Lord and
> Savior Jesus Christ. (NIV 2011)

How does a person pursue endurance? I'm sure there is more than one way. We can actively look for ways to endure. We can intentionally persevere and recognize situations where we know we will have to do just that. However, what I would like to encourage us all to do in pursuing endurance is to take a risk. Our international director encourages us, before filling out our ministry plan for the year, to make sure to include something that only God can do. When we attempt something beyond our comfort zone, bigger than we think we can do, I think we are pursuing endurance. We know we will be tempted to give up. It will take work to persevere.

When I started thinking about writing a book, I was scared. As I was writing, there were times I wanted to give up. Even when I was getting ready to send it in to see if it might be publishable, my finger hovered over the send button. What if it was rejected? What if all that work I put into it was in vain? What if I failed?

When it came time for our move to South Asia, I knew there would be culture shock. It was going to be hot. I was going to get sick. I wouldn't know the language or how to get around. I would have to go back to cooking from scratch. What if I couldn't make it? What if I failed? What if others saw weaknesses in me because I wouldn't be working in an area I knew well? What if . . .?

I think "what if" might be two of the scariest and most dangerous words in the English language. They keep us focused on ourselves and prevent us from dreaming and pursuing our dreams. We need to get rid of those two words and replace them with two other words: "pursue endurance."

As you think about what you would like to see happen in your part of the world and what your role might be, what dreams do you have? Is there anything you would like to pursue but have been too afraid to try? Think and pray about taking a risk. Trust God. Give yourself an opportunity to pursue endurance.

In all honesty we will not be able to pursue endurance if we are not in regular contact with the source of encouragement and endurance—God himself through his word.

Questions:
What is one dream that you have been afraid to pursue?

What can churches do to encourage cross-cultural workers to dream and pursue their vision but to also brace for the sometimes harsh realities of cross-cultural living?

Resource:
Ruth Ann Graybill, *The Emotional Needs of Women on the Mission Field* (La Mirada, CA: Biola Counseling Center, n.d.), http://www.mrnet.org/system/files/library/emotional_needs_of_women_on_mission_field.pdf.

Jars of Clay

The opposite of persevering is losing heart, giving up. I remember in sixth grade gym class we had to run a mile. I started off well, but in a matter of seconds I was far behind everyone else. I was so embarrassed that I tried to act like it didn't matter to me and went even slower than I had to! I lost heart, gave up, and didn't persevere in the race.

What can make you feel like giving up? What is it that discourages you and makes you lose heart?

In 2 Corinthians chapter 4 Paul, who had every opportunity to lose heart through the trials and difficulties he experienced, shares why he didn't lose heart. Look at verses 1–18:

> Therefore, since through God's mercy we have this ministry, we do not lose heart. Rather, we have renounced secret and shameful ways; we do not use deception, nor do we distort the word of God. On the contrary, by setting forth the truth plainly we commend ourselves to everyone's conscience in the sight of God. And even if our gospel is veiled, it is veiled to those who are perishing. The god of this age has blinded the minds of unbelievers, so that they cannot see the light of the gospel that displays the glory of Christ, who is the image of God. For what we preach is not ourselves, but Jesus Christ as Lord, and ourselves as your servants for Jesus' sake. For God, who said, "Let light shine out of darkness," made his light shine in our hearts to give us the light of the knowledge of God's glory displayed in the face of Christ.

But we have this treasure in jars of clay to show that this all-surpassing power is from God and not from us. We are hard pressed on every side, but not crushed; perplexed, but not in despair; persecuted, but not abandoned; struck down, but not destroyed. We always carry around in our body the death of Jesus, so that the life of Jesus may also be revealed in our body. For we who are alive are always being given over to death for Jesus' sake, so that his life may also be revealed in our mortal body. So then, death is at work in us, but life is at work in you.

It is written: "I believed; therefore I have spoken." Since we have that same spirit of faith, we also believe and therefore speak, because we know that the one who raised the Lord Jesus from the dead will also raise us with Jesus and present us with you to himself. All this is for your benefit, so that the grace that is reaching more and more people may cause thanksgiving to overflow to the glory of God.

Therefore we do not lose heart. Though outwardly we are wasting away, yet inwardly we are being renewed day by day. For our light and momentary troubles are achieving for us an eternal glory that far outweighs them all. So we fix our eyes not on what is seen, but on what is unseen, since what is seen is temporary, but what is unseen is eternal.

First of all we see that Paul did not lose heart because God's mercy sustained him. Paul recognized that it was because of God's mercy that he even had a ministry. He wasn't using deception in sharing the word of God; he was open and forthright in presenting truth. He didn't lose heart because he recognized the spiritual battle he was in as he shared light in the midst of darkness. He knew who his enemy was. He continued to preach the gospel and was dependent on God to allow the light to shine into the darkness. I think he recognized that results were not dependent on him, but on the Lord. He was faithful in preaching the gospel fully and truthfully.

What an awesome privilege it was to share the amazing truth of God's light with those around us. An especially thrilling moment for me was when I shared the gospel with my neighbor and she said in response to it, "I've never heard that before." This light that shines so brightly in the darkest corners of the world—the knowledge of the glory of God in the face of Christ—is indeed a most glorious message.

In contrast to the magnificent message, its messengers are merely jars of clay: common, quirky, feeble, mortal sinners like us who are saved by grace! This treasure is in normal, everyday clay—sometimes called cracked pots. Because of this, whenever someone comes to faith or God uses us in ministry, all the glory goes to him! Paul reminds us in 1 Corinthians 1 that God purposefully calls the weak, the poor, and the needy to himself so that he receives the glory. Paul recognized the importance of this and says later in 1 Corinthians 2:4,5: "My message and my preaching were not with wise and persuasive words, but with a demonstration of the Spirit's power, so that your faith might not rest on human wisdom, but on God's power."(NIV 2011)

And again in 2 Corinthians 12:7–10 Paul recounts:

> To keep me from becoming conceited, I was given a thorn in my flesh, a messenger of Satan, to torment me. Three times I pleaded with the Lord to take it away from me. But he said to me, "My grace is sufficient for you, for my power is made perfect in weakness." Therefore I will boast all the more gladly about my weaknesses, so that Christ's power may rest on me. That is why, for Christ's sake, I delight in weaknesses, in insults, in hardships, in persecutions, in difficulties. For when I am weak, then I am strong. (NIV 2011)

I dislike weakness. I want to appear strong, spiritual, and capable to others. I don't think I'm alone in this. From the results of a survey I sent out to women in cross-cultural ministry, some women were surprised by the masks people can wear on teams. There is sometimes a fear of sharing weaknesses or struggles because team-mates might think us unspiritual. However, I think it is essential for our own health and the health of our teams that we share our strug-gles openly and honestly, and that we love and pray for each other. In my own experience, I tried to keep a mask on in the beginning, but it was too hard. I needed the others on my team to know me, to understand who I was and where I was struggling. I needed their help. I don't think I ever felt judged when I shared my weaknesses or struggles. I felt loved, understood, supported, and encouraged.

It is when we recognize our weakness and our utter dependence on the Lord that we know he is the only one worthy of honor and glory. He is the one who sees us through. At the time, it may feel that we are on our own and it takes every ounce of strength to hold on. But as time passes and we look back at those times, we can see the hand of God and how he empowered us.

Paul saw that. He and his coworkers were pressed, perplexed, persecuted, and struck down. But they were never crushed, desper-ate, abandoned, or destroyed. In their bodies they carried the death of Jesus so that his life could also be revealed in them and in those around them. The same power that God used to raise Jesus from the dead will also raise us up with Jesus so that the grace that is reaching more and more people may cause thanksgiving to overflow for the glory of God.

Because of this power that is available to us and because it causes grace to reach more and more people for God's glory, Paul again writes that we don't have to lose heart! He recognizes that we might be wasting away physically, but spiritually we can be growing stronger. Paul contrasts the difference between the tempo-ral hardships with the eternal glory that is far more important and worthwhile. This eternal perspective kept Paul from losing hope. We, too, need to keep that eternal perspective in order to persevere.

There is a famous sermon entitled "It's Friday, but Sunday's Comin'." (You can watch a video clip online at http://www.youtube.com/watch?v=YByT6wfdhJs.) Imagine the disciples and how they felt when Jesus died. It seemed their world had ended. Yet Jesus told them he would rise again. They needed to focus on eternity, not their present circumstances.

It may seem like Friday to you, but Sunday is coming. Keeping an eternal perspective is necessary when persevering.

Paul encourages his readers not to throw away their confidence, saying, "You need to persevere." The day is coming when we will receive what was promised, and until then we have the privilege of walking and persevering by faith.

Sometimes I think we grow discouraged, lose heart, and feel like quitting because we expect more of ourselves than is humanly possible. I'm not sure why, but there is a "superwoman" mentality in our line of work that is dangerous.

Sometimes we could work harder—I know that is true of me. I have the tendency to want to play before working! Other times I think we are expecting ourselves to do what only God can do. We cannot convince other women to trust Christ. We cannot save them. We cannot be perfect, know everything, and do everything. We are not omniscient. Have you ever felt guilty for not knowing everything? I have.

Several years ago I headed a committee planning a consultation. I was feeling afraid, a bit overwhelmed and discouraged. And it hit me that I was taking over God's role and forgetting my own. I was not capable to work in people's hearts or cause them to come. I did not have ultimate control over venues and circumstances. So I came up with a three-sentence motto to help me remember to do what I can and trust God to do what he does:

1. *Do the possible.* We put on the armor of God. We feed ourselves spiritually. We do what we can. We visit. We share. We pray. We proclaim. We give. We teach. We model. We encourage others.

2. *Trust God with the impossible.* We entrust to God what we cannot do on our own. We give situations to him, people to him, visa approvals to him, results to him, our own weaknesses to him for him to work through, souls for him to save.
3. *Don't confuse the two.* We don't do God's job and he doesn't do ours. We are faithful. We grow. We learn. However, we are limited, finite humans. God is God. We are not. Let's not get confused on who is who.

Remember, we are jars of clay: common, everyday, sometimes fragile clumps of dirt. But the message that we hold inside—the living water that is needed by people everywhere—is amazing, glorious, and life changing.

I once saw a clay pot at the top of Mt. Nebo in Jordan. It was there for thirsty, parched, weary travelers. It was not a beautiful pot. No one would look at it and want it for a home decoration. But it was indeed a beautiful thing for those needing what was inside it—for those who received life-giving water.

We may not be beautiful pots. We may be weak, common, and ordinary, but it is when we are weak that we are strong, because God is the one who works through us. As a result he will receive the glory for any good that happens, for needs that are met. And that is how it should be. May God protect us from thinking that it is the pot that is all important! This pot will break apart, but the glory that is inside will live on. To God be the glory.

Questions:

How have you seen God work through you as his "jar of clay"?

How can a more safe and open atmosphere be developed in your church where cross-cultural workers feel even freer to share their struggles and challenges without fear of losing support?

Resource:

Sue Eenigenburg and Robynn Bliss, *Expectations and Burnout: Women Surviving the Great Commission* (Pasadena: William Carey Library, 2010).

Living Hope, Eternal Inheritance, and Refined Faith

When my grandpa passed away, my grandma was downsizing and asked me if there was anything I would like that belonged to them. When I was a little girl, I loved playing on their stairs, and at the bottom of those stairs was a little ceramic dog. I would pretend the dog was real and pet it. Sometimes I talked to it as I held it. My grandma had around fifteen grandchildren who ran up and down the stairs, and the dog would faithfully sit at the bottom through all our activities, which sometimes included chasing each other up and down the stairs or sliding down them on our bottoms! I had such good memories of that little dog figurine that I asked if I might have that. She said yes and saved it for me. I delighted in this inheritance!

When we moved back to the States, the ceramic dog came to live with us. I don't know how long my grandparents had that little statue, but I know it had to be at least thirty years. It was so fun to see him once again as I placed him at the bottom of our stairs, and he sat there as my four children—their great grandchildren—ran up and down. We had had him a few years when my youngest accidentally kicked him while running and pieces broke off the side of his face. We glued him back together the best we could and placed his bad side (since it looked like something from a horror movie!) away from public viewing!

I didn't want my daughter to feel bad because it was an accident, but I was really sad. That dog held such special memories for me that it was hard to see him so mutilated! When we were preparing to move back overseas, he was really too broken to put in storage or take with us, so I decided to throw him away.

That earthly inheritance did not last. However, Peter tells us that our inheritance that comes from God will never break, fade, or perish. It is eternal.

Let's look together at 1 Peter 1:3–9:

> Praise be to the God and Father of our Lord Jesus Christ! In his great mercy he has given us new birth into a living hope through the resurrection of Jesus Christ from the dead, and into an inheritance that can never perish, spoil or fade. This inheritance is kept in heaven for you, who through faith are shielded by God's power until the coming of the salvation that is ready to be revealed in the last time. In this you greatly rejoice, though now for a little while you may have had to suffer grief in all kinds of trials. These have come so that the proven genuineness of your faith—of greater worth than gold, which perishes even though refined by fire—may result in praise, glory and honor when Jesus Christ is revealed. Though you have not seen him, you love him; and even though you do not see him now, you believe in him and are filled with an inexpressible and glorious joy, for you are receiving the end result of your faith, the salvation of your souls.

Praise God that in his mercy he gave us a new birth into a living hope because Jesus rose from the dead. Because of this new birth and being born into the family of God, we have an inheritance that is secure. It can never be taken away; it will never spoil or disappear. It is kept securely in heaven for us, and we are shielded by God's power until that day when we live with him in glory.

I like this picture of being shielded by God's power (v. 5). We are guarded, protected, kept safe by the power of God. What a wonderful picture for those who are undergoing persecution! What security we have in knowing that we are being protected until we are at home with him! Nothing can separate us from God, because it is his power that is protecting us. We can rejoice in that.

Picture a dad going into a swimming pool with his daughter. He is holding her in his arms, and the tips of her toes barely touch the water. At first she is a little frightened, but gradually she relaxes. Then he steps in a little deeper and the water is up to her little knees. She clings tighter to his neck and he can feel her tense up, but in time she realizes that he is not going to let her go and she relaxes a bit. After some time, he steps a little further into the pool and the water is now up past her waist. She screams and tries to hold on even tighter to her dad. The water is higher and she is more scared. Her dad continues to hold onto her, and she senses that his hold has not slackened and she is still safely in his arms. So she stops squirming and clinging so tightly. He goes further and she feels the water going up to her neck. She starts to feel a bit panicky and holds on even tighter while crying. But he talks softly to her and tells her he will keep her safe. She can trust him. She feels his arms around her, she remembers how he has kept her safe, and she trusts him.

Now the thing the little girl doesn't know is this: the entire time she's been in her daddy's arms, the water has been over her head. She was in peril as soon as they stepped into the pool. Had it not been for her dad, she would have been in imminent danger from the very beginning. The only thing keeping her safe the entire time has been her dad. It's just that the deeper she and her dad went into the water, the more she *thought* she was in danger. Her situation never really changed. She was constantly in danger. It was her father who was always keeping her safe.

The same is true of us. It is always our Father who is keeping us safe. There are times we feel like we are in more danger or times when we feel that we are safer. The truth is that we are always safely and securely cared for by God's power.

Does this mean we are forever safe from trials or troubles? Is that the kind of protection we have? No, because the very next verse (v. 6) points out that "though now for a little while you may have had to suffer grief in all kinds of trials." It is a protection that sees us through trials, not necessarily protects us from trials. Could he protect us from trials? Sure he could, and sometimes he does. But one of the reasons he allows us to persevere through them is so that our faith—which is more precious and valuable than even gold, one of the most valuable things on earth—could be proved genuine and result in glory and honor coming to Jesus Christ.

Read Psalm 91. Look carefully at verse 15 where the psalmist says of the Lord, "I will be with him in trouble." How does God protect us from, as well as during, times of trial?

Discussing how God protects from and through usually reminds me of Hebrews chapter 11. These heroes all had faith, but their stories are vastly different. In the first half are those who had faith and were delivered from the mouths of lions, received their dead back alive, and escaped the power of the sword. In the second half are those who had faith and were put to death, flogged, chained, and imprisoned. They all had faith, and God was working through each life in a way that would bring him the most glory. Remember in the book of Acts where James was killed and Peter was delivered? Why? They both had faith. I'm sure believers were praying for them both. God's protection is so powerful it not only protects from, but also protects through every kind of danger. And the end result in believers is a faith that is priceless!

Gold, though precious and refined by fire, will still perish one day. Our faith, when it is refined by trials, will prove genuine and result in eternal glory for God.

Peter goes on to describe how those of us who have not seen Jesus still love him and believe in him and so are filled with an inexpressible and glorious joy because we know our souls are saved. Sure, we know that in the short term there may be pain, but in the long run our eternal salvation is worth it! We are saved and our Savior is glorified. What a perfect ending—or really, what a perfect beginning of all eternity.

In 1 Peter 2:20–23, Peter goes on to encourage believers who were suffering by letting them know whose example they were following when they suffered for doing good:

> But how is it to your credit if you receive a beating for doing wrong and endure it? But if you suffer for doing good and you endure it, this is commendable before God. To this you were called, because Christ suffered for you, leaving you an example, that you should follow in his steps.

> "He committed no sin, and no deceit was found in his mouth."

> When they hurled their insults at him, he did not retaliate; when he suffered, he made no threats. Instead, he entrusted himself to him who judges justly.

And again in 1 Peter 4:19: "So then, those who suffer according to God's will should commit themselves to their faithful Creator and continue to do good."

When we suffer we must follow the example of Jesus and entrust ourselves to God. As this trust—this faith—is proved genuine and real, it will bring Jesus glory.

I like how Peter contrasts the perishable versus the imperishable in his writing. Our salvation is sure and our inheritance is imperishable; gold, silver, and things of this world are perishable. I cannot find M&M's in South Asia, so I always bring a few bags from the States as a treat. I was saving a bag for a special occasion and soon that occasion arrived. I opened the bag and what was inside did not resemble M&M's at all! It was just a bag of melted, jumbled, pale brown, smashed orbs. What a disappointment! As valuable and good as things of this world can be, they will not last. Peter talks in 1 Peter 1:17–19, 23 that we were saved by the precious blood of Christ and born again of a seed that is imperishable through the living and enduring word of God:

Since you call on a Father who judges each person's work
impartially, live your time as foreigners here in reverent
fear. For you know that it was not with perishable things
such as silver or gold that you were redeemed from the
empty way of life handed down to you from your ances-
tors, but with the precious blood of Christ, a lamb without
blemish or defect . . . For you have been born again, not
of perishable seed, but of imperishable, through the living
and enduring word of God.

We are eternally secure. We are eternally loved. We are valued
by God. We are also given opportunities in this life for our faith to
grow, and to glorify God as we demonstrate to the world and to Jesus
that it is genuine. Trials should not influence our faith; rather our
faith should influence how we persevere through our trials!

Remember, this life is the only opportunity we have to walk by
faith. One day we will see him. One day we will walk by sight. For
now, in this adventurous journey, we love him and believe in him
though we don't see him. We walk by faith, even through trials, for
the glory of Jesus.

Questions:
What was especially meaningful to you from Psalm 91?

How can the church help spiritually nurture the worker when she is
overseas?

Resource:
Peter's Wife is a newsletter for women who work across cultures.
Write to Diane at the following email address: Peter_s_Wife@mail.
vresp.com.

III.
Joy in Stretching Spiritually

Sometimes in the midst of ministry I have wondered what I am doing. It often doesn't look how I pictured it. In the midst of all there is to do, it is easy to lose sight of the big picture, of seeing the big cathedral when I am just a brick layer.

In the midst of many different roles, I have wondered if I've handled any of them well. Being a foreign woman in a culture where women aren't valued has made me question my worth. Wanting to be a godly Christian woman in a place where people assumed I was like the "Christian" women on American soap operas left me feeling wrongly judged and forlorn. As a married couple (and I think I can safely speak for my husband in this instance!) we've experienced culture stress and have seen it attack our marriage. It's hard enough being a wife and mother, but having those roles in a different culture makes it even tougher. Desiring to be fruitful and faithful causes us to live with tension in the realm of choosing to continue on despite obstacles and the need for hard work (to cultivate faithfulness) or trying something different or work hard somewhere else (to cultivate fruitfulness). How can we know which God wants us to do? How can we cultivate both? The one phrase that comes to mind in these struggles is "there ain't nothin' easy!"

However, it can be easy to grow discontented and wonder if I've made a terrible mistake and could have done so much more if I had stayed in my home country where I knew the language and culture and it took less time to simply live.

The good thing about these struggles and insecurities is that they cause us to lean on our Savior to make it through each day. Through them there is spiritual growth, a need to cling to the vine (John 15) and abide in him, because we come to realize we can do nothing on our own.

There is a lot to learn in ministry. Working across cultures is an excellent school for learning lessons we need to know in order to grow in fruitfulness and faithfulness.

I recently read about the second half of life in ministry in *Live Like You Mean It*. Addington writes, "Almost everyone who does not finish well fails in the second half of life" (2010, p. 53). That gave me pause as I am definitely in the second half of life and I want to finish well.

Without perseverance, finishing well is impossible. I want to take to heart Paul's writing in Galatians 6:9, "Let us not become weary in doing good, for at the proper time we will reap a harvest if we do not give up."

On the following pages are a few stories that illustrate how God has been at work in me. By God's grace I determine in my heart to not grow weary, but to finish well.

As the Deer

For me, becoming a cross-cultural worker was a lot like a trip I took as a child to a deer-petting farm. While growing up, I would get several new outfits whenever my family would take a vacation. One year I got a cute little short set with a blue top that had layers of ruffles. That year one of our stops was a deer-petting farm. They gave us a package of what looked like graham crackers and told us to keep moving as we fed the deer. I enjoyed walking among these beautiful creatures and feeding them. Soon I ran out of food and, at the same time, I forgot to keep moving.

The deer gathered around and, before I knew what was happening, they had begun to eat my shirt. I watched with alarm layer after layer of ruffles disappearing. I remember standing there calling for help and probably crying, unsure of what to do as my decorative ruffles were being eaten away. I think it was my sister who came over, got me moving again, and shooed all the deer away.

In moving overseas, away from my comfort zones and all that was familiar, layer after layer of my sense of spirituality was being stripped away. I didn't think I was an angry person, yet I struggled with anger. I thought I was a spiritually mature person, yet I began to see that I didn't know God as well as I thought I did. I thought my marriage was strong and found it shaken. The love that I had felt for these people I had never met turned at times into dislike once I got to know them. All that I learned in Bible school was helpful, but paled in comparison to what I needed for daily survival. I had been ready to change the world and discovered that I was the one who needed to be changed.

Of course, the deer analogy only goes so far. There was no useful purpose in losing the ruffles off of my shirt . . . except to feed the deer! However, God had a definite purpose in stripping away the layers of my false sense of spirituality. He replaced every flimsy layer of character or spirit that was mere decoration with a firm foundation that has made me more able to withstand anything trying to eat away at my life.

I am so thankful that Jesus Christ saved me as a young teen. He changed my life and gave me the desire to serve him wholeheartedly. I am also thankful that he rescued me once again as a woman in ministry. It has been a painful, joyous, dreadful, awesome, terrible, wonderful, failing, successful, amazing process in which his strength has been seen in my weakness. His power has been evident as he gave me grace in the midst of overcoming temptation. His love has transformed my apathy, and his faithfulness has shined through my own faithlessness.

By the time those deer left, I had only a few layers of ruffles left, yet in my life I seem to have a never-ending supply of ruffles that God brings to light and works to remove. I am thankful he continues his work in me.

Questions:
What has God stripped away from your life as you've lived overseas, and what has he added?

What can the church do to help provide stability for the worker who is experiencing almost constant change?

Resource:
Thrive Ministry retreat: http://thriveministry.org

The Miraculous and the Mundane

Ramadan was almost over. There were more beggars on the street than normal. It was always so hard to know to whom to give. We met so many poor people, and we heard from our national friends that many of the beggars were wealthier than those who worked. We read accounts of beggars who would rent children to make more money or go to places for their bodies to be twisted or hurt so they could look worse and thus make more money. We tried to only give to those in our neighborhood, and we usually gave clothing or food, not money.

I saw two women begging as they walked together with their children near my house. I thought, "I have some clothes my kids have outgrown that would fit their children. I could give those to them, but also tell them why I am giving. I will tell them of the love of the Messiah as I reach out to them in love." I told the women to wait a few minutes, ran up to the apartment, and put clothes for each of their children in a bag. I quickly came down the stairs and walked up to the two ladies to give them the bag. Just as I was opening my mouth to tell them of the love of the Lord, each woman grabbed one side of the bag and they began to yell at each other, each one saying that the bag was for her only. They pulled and yelled and continued to fight as I tried to explain that because they were friends I had put enough for all their children in one bag. They ignored me, and I knew that I would not get to speak of the love of Jesus that day. They continued fighting over the bag as they moved on down the street.

Well that certainly didn't go as planned, and it certainly didn't provide an opportunity to talk about love! I had expected them to wait for the bag as I shared with them about the love of God. They would then take the bag gratefully and walk away more aware of who God is and why Jesus came to this earth.

How many ministry opportunities have not gone as expected? As a matter of fact, life as a cross-cultural worker isn't what I thought it would be. After reading biographies and hearing speakers, I was prepared for the miraculous. No one mentioned the mundane. When we lived overseas I could be doing laundry in the morning and sharing the gospel with a neighbor in the afternoon. I would cook dinner for the family and help the kids with homework one evening and go out visiting national friends another. When we were based in the States, I would find myself in England one week planning a conference on reaching unreached people groups, and the next week I would find myself mopping the floor in Pennsylvania.

Cross-cultural ministry is filled with the miraculous and the mundane, with opportunities to share the gospel with a person who has never heard it before and opportunities to serve by cleaning house and washing dishes. The wonderful thing about it is that God is not just interested in the miraculous—miracles are easy for him! He wants me to see how he can teach me or use me to reflect his glory as I do the mundane.

Giving a bag of clothes to beggar women turned out to be a mundane event; it could maybe even be seen as a failure. However, who knows? It could have ended up miraculous. What if they had heard? What did they think of my actions and theirs later that night? Did they hear anything I said? Who else has come into their lives since then? I don't know the answers, but I won't stop trying to reach out in love even when the results are not what I expected. I will persevere with the mundane while I wait for the miracles to happen. They might not come the expected way, but would they be miracles if they did?

Questions:
How do you handle the mundane when you sometimes desire only miracles?

What are some good debriefing questions to ask cross-cultural workers to get a better idea of their life and ministry?

Resource:
Read the article "What Missionaries Ought to Know about Debriefing": http://www.missionarycare.com/brochures/br_debriefing.htm.

Fasting with Donuts

I was dealing with a difficult issue. I can't even remember what the issue was, but I do remember being challenged to fast and pray about it. I believe this was the first time I had ever fasted, and I was very excited about it. It seemed like such a spiritual thing to do. Sad to say, at that time I had been a believer for over eighteen years and had never fasted before.

That morning I got up and didn't eat. I spent time in prayer. That afternoon I had arranged to meet with a friend and we were out walking. She needed to pick up some things, so we stopped in one of our favorite stores. The reason it was one of our favorite shops is that occasionally it would have something new to the city that we could normally only find in the States. It may have been a brand of cereal, a special candy, or a type of snack.

As we were walking through the store, we saw an item we had never seen in our host city before. We saw donuts! And not just any donuts—these had chocolate icing! What a wonderful surprise. We bought a package to share and couldn't wait to taste them. As soon as we had paid for them and stepped outside, we tore open the package and I took my first bite.

My first thought was, "Wow! These are incredible!"

My second thought was, "Oh, no! I'm fasting!"

My friend took one look at my face and knew something was wrong, and she knew me well enough to know it wasn't the donut! She asked me what it was. I looked at the donut with a big bite taken out of it, and then I looked at her. "I'm fasting," I said. She looked confused, since everyone knows (even those new to the world of fasting) that donuts aren't a part of fasting.

So I was fasting up until that moment when I saw a donut and lost my head. What does one do when one is fasting but has just forgotten and taken a bite of food?

Since this was my first time, I wasn't sure. Do I spit it out? That would have been hard to do since that bite of donut went through my lips and down my throat rather quickly. Do I just forget the fast, since I'd already broken it, and finish the donut? Is there an "oops" moment when you can tell God you are sorry you forgot you were fasting and continue on from there as if that bite never took place? I'm not sure there is an answer for that!

I have fasted more times since then, praying for God to work in miraculous ways in people's lives and in ministry. However, whenever I fast I almost always experience a craving for a donut!

Questions:
What are the scriptural guidelines for fasting?

Set aside a time of fasting and prayer for ministry breakthroughs for the workers you support.

Resource:
Elmer L. Towns, *Fasting for Spiritual Breakthrough: A Guide to Nine Biblical Fasts* (Ventura, CA: Regal Books, 1996).

Trees or Football

When visiting India, I was amazed at brightly colored saris hanging from roofs, huge bulls wandering the streets, and the strength and stamina of rickshaw drivers. The food is spicy. The weather is hot. It didn't take long to realize that I love fans, inverters, and reverse osmosis-filtered water! One of the worst feelings in the world is when the fan stops working because the electricity goes out just when you are beginning to feel cool, and sweat begins to stream out of every pore. Internet access is never taken for granted.

Monkeys are no longer cute animals to see at a zoo. They are scavengers who roam the streets looking for fruit to steal or strangers to threaten. Monkeys are also animals to be worshiped. This was one of the hardest parts of our visit to India. I was watching people go to temples dedicated to worshiping monkeys, bringing offerings and burning incense to these creatures. I saw bulls with garlands around their necks and horns, being regarded as sacred idols. But worse than this to me was seeing people bow down, circling round and round, worshiping trees.

I was appalled. How could anyone worship a tree? Words from Isaiah 44:15–17 struck home forcefully when I read about trees:

> It is man's fuel for burning; some of it he takes . . . and bakes bread. But he also fashions a god and worships it; he makes an idol and bows down to it. Half of the wood he burns in the fire; over it he prepares his meal, he roasts his meat and eats his fill. He also warms himself and says, "Ah! I am warm; I see the fire." From the rest he makes a god, his idol; he bows down to it and worships. He prays to it and says, "Save me! You are my god!"

I wanted to go up to those dear people and tell them, "Stop it! It is just a tree. It was created by the Creator. Worship him. This is just a tree!"

As I returned home and was pondering these idols and idolatrous people who worshiped them, I thought about how glad I was that I did not worship monkeys, cows, or trees. Idolatry was hideous to me. I kept picturing these people around the tree and detested their worship of it.

God, in his mercy, reminded me that not all idols are visible. They are not all animals or things made of gold, silver, or wood. A friend, an experienced worker in India, brought this home to me as I was talking with her about all I had seen in India and how I wanted to go up to these people and say, "It is just a tree!" She told me of her experience of living in America: when football season was in full swing and the Super Bowl was anxiously anticipated, she felt like saying to people, "It is just a football!"

Ouch! That hit home. I realized that in America I may not have physical, tangible idols that people see me bowing down to. My idols may be invisible. They are what I spend the most time doing, what I love the most. What do I worship that others cannot see? Do I worship pleasure, position, power, or possessions . . . or anything else that might not start with the letter *p*?

I need not be so judgmental, arrogant, or dismissive of people worshiping trees when they could rightfully say to me, "It is just a television." "It is just a novel." "It is just . . ." My problem is I can fill in the blank of what I worship with more than just a tree.

It isn't just a tree; it's anything that captures our hearts and pulls us away from the one true God who is worthy of all our worship.

Questions:

What idols are you aware of in your life, and what do you need to do about them?

What are some idols that people in your culture worship? What do you know about the idols in other countries? How can churches and cross-cultural workers dethrone idols?

Resource:

Kelly Minter, *No Other Gods: Confronting Our Modern Day Idols* (Colorado Springs: Cook, 2008).

People Who Live with Glass Tabletops Shouldn't . . .

We were getting our apartment ready so that we could move in. After months of living with other people, it was going to be great to have our own place again! The apartment was empty except for a bed and a lovely glass-topped dining room table that our landlord was nice enough to let us use. Both were stored in bedrooms, and I suggested we move the table into the dining room since the landlord and his extended family were coming over that night for a time of fellowship, prayer, and dedication of the flat.

The table's wrought iron legs held a beautiful glass pane with delicate etchings around the edges. Our landlord's brother was going to sell it, but our landlord liked it so much he was keeping it.

As we were preparing to move it, I asked Don, "Is the glass attached?" He tried lifting it off, and it seemed securely attached to the legs. He then began to show me how we needed to lift the table and turn it on its side so that we could get it through the door and into the dining room.

As soon as we started to tilt it, we learned that the glass wasn't as securely attached as we thought. We saw the pane slide off and then hit the tile floor, shattering into thousands of pieces. The shards of glass exploded into several rooms as the sound echoed all around us like a bomb blast.

We stood there in silence, unable to believe what had just happened. You know those moments when you know something just happened, and it even seemed to happen in slow motion, and yet it doesn't seem like it should have happened?

What were we going to tell our landlord? Where would we put the snacks we had bought to serve the ten or so people who were coming over? Would we ever get all the glass swept up? How could I stop the cut on my leg from bleeding?

Well the landlord's main (and gracious) concern was that no one was injured. They invited us to their apartment for refreshments after a time of prayer in our place. We think we found all the glass pieces, and since I had brought a small first-aid kit with us for our move, we were able to put it to use right away.

It took some time, but we finally found a shop that would make us a new glass tabletop. Don ordered it, and it was delivered in just a few days. It wasn't long after that Don noticed the glass was put on upside down and needed to be turned over. At this point we were thankful it wasn't attached, and we were very, very careful!

Questions:

What are a few of the typical challenges you have faced working across cultures after moving to your new country?

What are some of the challenges you think cross-cultural workers face in their ministry?

Resource:

Lois A. Dodds and Lawrence E. Dodds, *Stressed from Core to Cosmos: Issues and Needs Arising from Cross-cultural Ministry* (Liverpool, PA: Heartstream Resources, 1997), http://www.heart-streamresources.org/media/CORE2COS.pdf.

Remember Jeremiah 29:11

We were on a plane in a row with three seats. Don was by the window, I was in the middle, and I watched to see who my seatmate would be. I always try to guess just by looking. I usually pray for opportunities to witness on a plane. Sometimes (well, usually) opportunities seem scarce. Often the person next to me doesn't seem to want to talk. On one flight the woman next to me kept a blanket over her head the entire time!

I saw a fortyish woman with short hair, carrying a backpack and looking for a seat. I thought it might be her and it was! She seemed very friendly and slightly inebriated. She pretty much threw herself in the seat next to me exclaiming, "Oh, I am *so* glad to get away. I had the longest weekend imaginable with my missionary parents. It feels so good to get away from them! Why can't they just be my parents without being missionaries? I mean, I love my parents, but just before I leave my dad says to me, 'Don't forget Jeremiah 29:11.' And of course I'm going to go look it up just to see what it says. But I am happy to be out of there."

When she stopped to take a breath, Don and I were looking at her with smiles. I said to her, "I'm not even going to tell you what we do." "OH NO!!" she yelled, "Does God have a sense of humor or what? I'm trying to get away from people like you, and where do I end up sitting? Right next to a younger version of my parents!"

Thus began one of my most enjoyable (and memorable) conversations on a plane! We talked about reentry, hypocrisy in the church, judgmental attitudes of Christians, grace, and truth. I told her stories of my kids' reentry back into U.S. culture, and she laughed and said she loved our kids! I told her how when my five-year-old daughter (who knew she was born in Dallas, had lived in Jordan, was now living in Egypt but flying to Ohio) was asked at the airport by a U.S. customs agent, "And where are you from?" she replied, "Now that's a good question!" Another time she was asked by fellow junior high students if she knew who Calvin Klein was. Trying to fake it she said, "I think my brother has one of his CDs." My seatmate was already shaking her head before I even finished the story, saying, "Oh no, don't try and fake it!" And I assured her that my daughter never tried to fake it again!

Now Don says my seatmate would have laughed at anything due to her intoxication, but I think she enjoyed the stories and could relate to them. She told me tales of her own reentry and how she didn't seem to fit in at school or church. She was lonely, and the American culture was so different from what she was used to. She found solace in music but, due to experiencing unwarranted judgment by lying church members, even that was taken away. She told me about her family, her parents' ministry, and her views of Jesus, God, the church, and ways to God. We talked about how the church views gay people and how Jesus views them. Every now and again when it seemed to fit I would quote her dad, "Well, don't forget Jeremiah 29:11." And she would laugh and give me a high five. We traded questions about life and ministry, culture and values, the Bible and its relevancy to life. The three hours flew by! I shared some TCK resources with her that she didn't even know existed. She said she knew of nothing like that for her when she came back to the States.

As the plane landed I told her I hoped it wasn't too painful sitting next to people like us, and she said she rather enjoyed it. It was a refreshingly open conversation. I was touched by her and her sincerity to live life well and to help others. She was honest, candid, and open to talking about difficult issues.

As we parted ways I prayed that she would look up Jeremiah 29:11 and recognize that no matter how the church had wronged her, no matter how her past had hurt her, no matter that she doesn't fit in any culture . . . God loves her and declares to her, "I know the plans I have for you, plans to prosper you and not to harm you, plans to give you hope and a future."

Questions:
What can we do to build into the lives of TCKs we know?

Do most people expect more from TCKs (MKs) than other children? Why or why not? And if so, how can you help TCKs in your church deal with unrealistic expectations?

Resource:
Joyce M. Bowers, ed., *Raising Resilient MKs: Resources for Caregivers, Parents, and Teachers* (Colorado Springs: Association of Christian Schools International, 1998), http://www.missionarycare. com/ebooks/Raising_Resilient_MKs.pdf.

IV
A Deeper Look at Joy

Is there really joy in being stretched spiritually? In being pushed outside of our comfort zones?

When we're being stretched, we need to keep our eyes on Jesus and in the truths of Scripture to make it through. I'm sure you have heard about the difference between joy and happiness. I don't want to belabor that point. But to recap, happiness is more dependent on circumstances and can ebb and flow. Joy is more dependent on abiding in Christ even though circumstances might be terrible.

There are some bitter cross-cultural workers. It seems they have forgotten how to forgive, how to share openly, and how to enjoy life. Past grievances, present distresses, and future worries weigh them down. Life is hard. Team life brings about many challenges and difficult discussions. When recalling life in our home countries, we often have "selective memory" as we only remember the good things. It's tempting to think it would be so much easier if we returned there. We watch our kids struggle. We hear from our aging parents. Visa issues surface. National friends seem to expect more or less but not what we think they want or need from us. When persecution comes, our national friends are treated much worse than we are. We wonder how to know when enough is enough.

How can a person have joy in the midst of such difficulties?

Let's investigate some scripture passages to see what God's word says about joy in the midst of challenges.

Joy in His Presence
(Mary)

There are many things in life that make me happy: a sunny day, a beautiful flower, a date with my husband. There are also many things in life that can make me sad: a sunny day (too hot to go outside), a beautiful flower (it won't stay that way; it will die soon), a date with my husband (who started that argument anyway?). It is easy to see that though things may sometimes cause happiness, they won't always bring lasting joy, nor can they ever guarantee it.

Some people may try to find joy in their possessions; others may seek it in their accomplishments. When my first book came out, it was really exciting to see it published. I searched the Internet for the title to see where the book was mentioned and if anything was written about it. I found mentions of it on several sites, but the most exciting one was at Deeper Roots Publications and—are you ready for this? —it was in the evangelism, missions, and heroes category. To think a book I had written was even *near* the heroes' category! I was amazed. I then searched for it on Amazon.com and found it! I was thrilled until I looked under author and it said "Unknown"! I'm still learning that true meaning and real joy in life are not about me and my accomplishments. My life is from God and for God. True joy is from him. I cannot look to my accomplishments to be my source for any lasting joy.

I remember, before I came to know Christ, thinking that if I could just look like this person or have the talents, abilities, or clothes of another person, then life would be good and I would be truly happy. Even now I sometimes find myself jealous of other people's spiritual gifts and discontent with my own, thinking that

if what I did was as important and influential as what they did, then
I would be happier. It is kind of like Christmas morning after the
packages are opened and wrapping paper is strewn on the floor;
there is sometimes a letdown feeling: "Is that all there is?" I may
have a lot, but there is always more I could have. Joy cannot be found
in what we own or what we do.

David wrote in Psalm 16:11, "You make known to me the path of
life; you will fill me with joy in your presence, with eternal pleasures
at your right hand." True and lasting joy is found in God's presence.
We see from this psalm and others that David discovered this joy in
God's presence. So did Mary. Read Luke 10:38–42:

> As Jesus and his disciples were on their way, he came to a
> village where a woman named Martha opened her home
> to him. She had a sister called Mary, who sat at the Lord's
> feet listening to what he said. But Martha was distracted
> by all the preparations that had to be made. She came to
> him and asked, "Lord, don't you care that my sister has
> left me to do the work by myself? Tell her to help me!"
>
> "Martha, Martha," the Lord answered, "you are worried
> and upset about many things, but few things are
> needed—or indeed only one. Mary has chosen what is
> better, and it will not be taken away from her."

Mary knew that true joy in life was not found in her accomplishments or activities, but in her relationship with Jesus Christ. She
would not allow herself to be distracted from her relationship with
the Lord by things to do.

I think she recognized that true joy was found in the Lord's
presence. After spending time with him, she was able to live more
intentionally for him. And as a result she wasn't tempted to substi-
tute the love she had for him with her love for serving him.

In the midst of our busy lives as ministers of the gospel, all that
we do we should seek to do for God's glory. There are things that
have to be done: language to study, people to visit, meals to cook,
correspondence to keep up with . . . the list seems never-ending.

If we let those things become the focal point, we lose our joy; we grow tired because we lose our focus on Jesus in the busyness of doing things. Even if we are serving the Lord in all that we do, without investing time in his presence even the ministry we love can become stale.

I've come to the conclusion that spending time with God is always a choice. When my kids were younger and I was busier in the home, it was more difficult to make time to spend with God. Having my quiet time when the kids were awake worked when they were quite small. Although I wouldn't necessarily call it a quiet time! Getting up early before the kids awoke worked when they were in school. Now that my kids are grown and married and off on their own, it isn't necessarily any easier to choose to spend time with God, even though I have more free time! It is still a choice. Is it easier to find the time? Yes, it is. Am I less distracted? Yes, I am. But I am amazed that it still takes conscious effort to set aside time to spend with the one who died for me!

Why is it so hard to do the most necessary thing as a believer? Seriously, I know I am in a spiritual battle. But maybe at times I am tempted to think I am strong enough to handle life on my own. It is so easy to see what needs to be done all around me, but it is often difficult to see my own spiritual neediness. Even when I am involved in ministry, serving God can keep me so preoccupied that I don't take time to more intimately get to know the one I serve.

It is easy for me, and maybe other believers as well, to become lazy, to live day to day on past victories, infrequent quiet times, and stale prayer lives. However, it isn't enough to merely preserve my spiritual life; I must be zealous in my pursuit of knowing God. In order to prosper spiritually—or in situations like ours where we are ministering across cultures, to even survive—I need to make my relationship with the Lord a top priority.

Mary spent time with the Lord and found joy in his presence. She did not try to find joy in her accomplishments or ministry to him. As a matter of fact, she faced the displeasure of her sister for choosing to sit at the feet of Jesus. Martha needed help and she couldn't help but think that Mary was wasting her time sitting when she should have been working. However, it was time well spent! As Mary intentionally pursued a relationship with the Lord by sitting at his feet to learn, she was also able to recognize that joy is not found in possessions.

Look at Mark 14:3–9:

> While he was in Bethany, reclining at the table in the home of Simon the Leper, a woman came with an alabaster jar of very expensive perfume, made of pure nard. She broke the jar and poured the perfume on his head.
>
> Some of those present were saying indignantly to one another, "Why this waste of perfume? It could have been sold for more than a year's wages and the money given to the poor." And they rebuked her harshly.
>
> "Leave her alone," said Jesus. "Why are you bothering her? She has done a beautiful thing to me. The poor you will always have with you, and you can help them any time you want. But you will not always have me. She did what she could. She poured perfume on my body beforehand to prepare for my burial. Truly I tell you, wherever the gospel is preached throughout the world, what she has done will also be told, in memory of her." (NIV 2011)

Jesus had been telling his disciples about his upcoming death. I'm not sure they caught on. I can picture them talking among themselves, "What does he mean by that?" I think that Mary, however, knew. She had taken the time to sit at his feet and listen to him. That is why she came to him and gave to him so freely of her precious possessions.

I cannot tell you how many times I have thought, "If we just had a little more money, I would feel safer, and because of that security I would be happier." In contrast, Mary had discovered that joy is not found in what she owned; joy is only found in the presence of the Lord.

Mary wanted to honor Jesus in some way. I can imagine her thinking about what she could do, and eventually she came up with a plan. She had some special perfume and she wanted to give it to Jesus. She took this expensive fragrance and anointed his head and feet as an act of love for him. She didn't think about what others might say or think about herself and the cost of her gift. She simply wanted to be in his presence and honor him.

As she anointed him, people were rebuking her. They scolded her for wasting money. Earlier she was scolded for wasting her time, and now she is in trouble again for wasting her resources! In chapter 26 of Matthew's Gospel he writes that the disciples themselves were indignant. She should have been thinking of the poor and all that the money could do for them . . . just imagine what all could be done with the equivalent of $15,000 to $20,000! Yet she broke it open and gave it all at this one special time to the Lord. He was so touched by her gift that he said that what she had done would be remembered wherever the gospel is preached. Rather than scold her, Jesus praised her and made sure that future generations would recognize what she did.

This gift that she gave the Lord could show us several things:

1. We see that her security was not based in what she owned, but in who she served. She gave what could have been her savings, something for a rainy day in uncertain times, trusting God rather than herself to provide for her.

2. We see that in her generosity she gave it all, holding nothing back.

3. We see her uninhibited worship as she lived for an audience of one, looking only to him for praise, not others. She was unfazed by their criticism; she looked to the Lord.

4. We also see the strength of her relationship with the Lord as she understood that he was going to die. She knew who he was and the sacrifice he was going to make. She was preparing his body for burial.

Though life brings about many changes, the source of our joy doesn't change. It is being in the presence of the Lord that brings joy, no matter our circumstances, our possessions, or our accomplishments.

A few years ago I was watching two of my friends deal with their husbands' cancer. I told Don that if that ever happened to us not to expect that I would hold up as well as these two dear ladies did. I would be a basket case. Not too long after that, Don went to the doctor and a "suspicious mass" was found that needed to be checked out. Does anyone ever have a mass that isn't suspicious? When Don was diagnosed with a tumor that the doctor assumed was malignant, I realized that my most precious possession was not anything I owned but it was my husband. During the time of his diagnosis, surgery, and waiting for results, I read this passage in Mark about Mary.

It was like God was asking me, "Where is your security? Is it in another person or in me? Will you give your husband to me?"

Some people's source of security can be in another person, their job, their home, their savings, or their routine. Eventually God is going to ask, "Will you let me be your source of security and trust me?" Mary did. She gave freely what could have been kept as security for her. She didn't keep some of it or give him just a little. She was showing him that she trusted fully in him, that her joy was in him, not her possessions.

My first instinct with Don was to hold him close to me and away from God, like he was mine. I was afraid and wasn't sure I trusted God with him. In reality, I was trying to protect him from God, because I wasn't sure what would God do. I wanted to hang on to him and my will for us rather than give it all to God and trust him. Don's response when he was telling me what the doctor said still has the power to thrill my soul: "Sue, I really want to honor God through this. Let's pray that I will glorify him." His heart for God was so evident. He wasn't holding on tightly to life. He knew his security was in the Lord. However, I remember asking him before praying,

"Can I also ask for healing?" Of course we can ask, but we must recognize that, no matter what the outcome, there is no security and no joy apart from knowing and trusting God.

As I read this passage about Mary, I realized that God was asking me to give Don to him, and because I knew the Lord, by his grace I was able to do so. We entrusted him and his "suspicious mass" to the Lord. I didn't become a basket case. God's grace is always enough. He doesn't give it beforehand, but he always gives it in time. We do thank God that the tumor wasn't cancerous and he did bring healing. Through this experience I grew in my faith; God helped me recognize him as my source of security and gave joy, even through the uncertainty as we waited for the test results. Our source of security and joy, God himself, was going to take care of us no matter what the results were.

Mary recognized that Jesus was worthy of her trust, that he was her ultimate security and her complete joy. Because she knew him she gave him her all. She had spent time with him and found joy in him, not her circumstances, her accomplishments, or her possessions.

Have you been finding joy in his presence, or have you let other things crowd out your time with him?

If you have lost your joy, is it possible it is because you haven't been spending precious and needed time in his presence where true and lasting joy is found? Are you looking elsewhere for your security and lasting joy? Have you been too busy accomplishing things for him? Have you been relying too heavily on your possessions?

There are days I miss spending time in God's presence. Some days I spend more time and other days I spend less. There are times when I just sit and feel thankful and enjoy a cup of tea, knowing that it was provided for me by him. I may look at a certain view in nature and think about how awesome our Creator is. I can read a chapter of scripture or meditate on one verse. Some days I don't particularly feel joyful. Some days I am totally hormonal and absolutely cranky. There is no magic formula that if you spend this much time with God you will get this much joy. We don't spend time with God just to get joy. Joy is a byproduct of spending time with God and learning to trust him. God is our joy. We must be careful not to want the gifts of God more than God himself, the giver of all that is good. There is no exchange rate. However, there is no other source of lasting joy apart from God.

There is joy in his presence.

Questions:

What are you tempted to hold onto too tightly, and what scripture passage encourages you to give it to the Lord?

How do churches decide where to invest their money in fulfilling the Great Commission? How is giving taught and practiced in your church?

Resource:

David Platt, *Radical: Taking Back Your Faith from the American Dream* (Colorado Springs: Multnomah Books, 2010).

The Joy of the Lord Is Your Strength (Nehemiah)

I think every person going into cross-cultural work should read and study the book of Nehemiah. It is one of my favorite books of the Bible. It is a story of a man of prayer who sees a huge need and, with God's help, seeks to meet it. He faces opposition, derision, fear, and harassment head on as he relies on God for strength and help. No matter the cost, he did what was right and sought to honor God with his actions as he righteously influenced his nation in obedience to God. Let's scan quickly through the book of Nehemiah:

1. In chapter 1 Nehemiah is living in a cross-cultural situation. He hears about the overwhelming need of his homeland; he is moved to tears and goes to God for help.

2. In chapter 2 we see that he uses his position and asks for help from the king, having done some planning for what had to be done and some praying for God's intervention and aid. He goes to Jerusalem to personally examine the damage and invite others to participate with him in building the walls. He faces this first hurdle as his enemies mock him and try to make him too afraid to work by charging him with rebelling against the king. Nehemiah keeps his eyes fixed on God and the task God had given him to do.

3. In chapter 3 we read about everyone—priests, men of Jericho, Tekoites, Gibeonites, Meronothites, goldsmiths, perfumers, city officials, Zanoahites, Levites, men of the valley, Shallum and his daughters, temple servants—working together to

rebuild the wall, laboring side by side because the task was bigger than any one person. They all have to work to see their goal accomplished. I love the diversity of people from all walks of life—perfumers, women, goldsmiths, and priests—working to complete the goal.

4. In chapter 4 we see enemies taunting, mocking, and demoralizing the workers and threatening the workers with violence. Yet again Nehemiah turns to God in prayer and encourages the workers to not be afraid but to trust the Lord. They continue to work but are also prepared for battle. They have a plan if they are attacked, but they do not stop their work because they knew, "Our God will fight for us!" (Nehemiah 4:19, NIV 2011)

5. In chapter 5 Nehemiah tackles an internal problem. Some people were so poor that they had sold their children to others as slaves in order to eat. Nehemiah angrily confronts the people about this evil and the people repent. Nehemiah goes above and beyond the call of duty and does not use the governor's allowance, even though he was entitled to it. He is generous as he invites many people to dine with him and only asks that God would remember him.

6. In chapter 6 the enemies seek to trick Nehemiah and deter him from the work. They use lies, innuendos, and threats to frighten him, but Nehemiah keeps to the task at hand and prays to the Lord for help and strength. He commits his enemies, those outside his camp, and those within, into the Lord's hands. They finish the wall, and everyone recognizes it was done with the help of God. Their enemies lose heart, but didn't totally give up.

7. In chapter 7 they post guards, recount the names of the people who had returned to Jerusalem, and determine who should be priests and who shouldn't be.

8. In chapter 8 the people gather to hear the word of the Lord read and explained, and it results in them worshiping God. The

people realize how sinful they are and as they worship feel convicted of their sin and begin weeping. Their leaders encourage them to not weep, but to rejoice that they understood the word of the Lord. They are told to celebrate because "the joy of the Lord is your strength." (Nehemiah 8:10, NIV 2011)

9. In chapter 9 they assemble with fasting and confess their sin as they continue to listen to the word of the Lord. They also begin praising God for all he had done for them and their forefathers; they determine to obey God and want to be held accountable, so they commit themselves in writing to follow the Lord.

10. In chapter 10 we see the names of all who signed the document, and the people agree together to follow God's word and to take care of the house of God.

11. In chapter 11 people come to live in the city and various roles are assigned to provide leadership.

12. In chapter 12 we see who the priests were and how people came to worship as they dedicated the wall to the Lord

13. In chapter 13 the people are continuing to listen as the Word is read and trying to follow through in obedience to what was written. Nehemiah had gone, and when he returns he sees some things being done wrong; he confronts the people, sets things right, and looks only to God for his reward.

I see a lot of similarities between rebuilding a wall and planting churches! The work is hard. Our coworkers come from different backgrounds and have different giftings. We all need to work together; the task is bigger than any one agency. Opposition and harassment are faced; we worship, we rejoice, we are sorrowful, we repent, we do right, we fail, we succeed, we are frightened, we grow tired, we keep working, we look to God.

Since there are a lot of similarities between our situation and Nehemiah's, I think we can learn from him. In the midst of the people's sorrow over their sin, Nehemiah told the people, "Do not grieve, for the joy of the Lord is your strength" (8:10). Let's focus on chapter 8.

The people had been working really, really hard. They were not getting enough sleep. They were emotionally drained as they faced opposition, fear, and harassment in the midst of their work. Some of the people working weren't really suited for the task at hand—what would a perfumer or a goldsmith know about building a wall? Yet they had a vision and kept working. When they finally finished their project, they had time to gather and to listen collectively to the word of the Lord. They realized, in the midst of their tiredness and weakness, that they hadn't been obeying the word of the Lord, and they couldn't stop crying because they felt such remorse.

Let's read what happened in 8:10:

> Nehemiah said, "Go and enjoy choice food and sweet drinks, and send some to those who have nothing prepared. This day is holy to our Lord. Do not grieve, for the joy of the Lord is your strength."

> The Levites calmed all the people, saying, "Be still, for this is a holy day. Do not grieve."

> Then all the people went away to eat and drink, to send portions of food and to celebrate with great joy, because they now understood the words that had been made known to them.

> On the second day of the month, the heads of all the families, along with the priests and the Levites, gathered around Ezra the teacher to give attention to the words of the Law. They found written in the Law, which the Lord had commanded through Moses, that the Israelites were to live in temporary shelters during the festival of the seventh month and that they should proclaim this word and spread it throughout their towns and in Jerusalem: "Go out into the hill country and bring back branches from olive and wild olive trees, and from myrtles, palms and shade trees, to make temporary shelters"—as it is written.

> So the people went out and brought back branches and
> built themselves temporary shelters on their own roofs, in
> their courtyards, in the courts of the house of God and in
> the square by the Water Gate and the one by the Gate of
> Ephraim. The whole company that had returned from exile
> built temporary shelters and lived in them. From the days
> of Joshua son of Nun until that day, the Israelites had not
> celebrated it like this. And their joy was very great.

Rather than letting the people continue in their sorrow, the leaders encouraged them to rejoice. They also encouraged them to obey Scripture and observe the Feast of Booths. And the people did so. They went out and found branches, remembered what God had done for their people in the past, and rejoiced as they never had as they obeyed God and found joy in it.

You have been working hard in the midst of difficult circumstances. You face difficulties, sorrows, and opposition. You don't do everything right. There are some scriptures that you are not obeying. God asks that we be holy as he is holy, and when we compare ourselves to his standards, we realize we fall far short. We need to grieve and to repent of our sin; we need to obey him in what we know to do. However, we also need to set aside time to rejoice—to recognize that the joy of the Lord is our strength.

What does it mean that the joy of the Lord is our strength?

There are several options; I think all of them are possible. Whatever gives God joy gives us strength. Joy produces strength. God himself is the source of our joy; we rejoice in the Lord, our source of strength.

God is indeed the source of our joy and our strength. When we rejoice in him, we have strength for whatever comes our way. When we rely on ourselves, or try to do things in our own power to create our own happiness, we are weakened and unable to live fully for the Lord. Joy is usually an outcome as we seek God; if we make joy our ultimate goal, it becomes illusive and often diminishes into happiness.

It is easy to get self-centered, to think our world revolves around us. We are tempted to think we are at the center of the universe and take our place on the throne! The danger for us as cross-cultural workers is that we are already in the midst of spiritual warfare simply because of living and ministering across cultures. When we become egocentric, our eyes are off of God and we relegate his call on our lives onto a back burner while we pursue our own dreams and possible delusions of grandeur. We share our vision with churches; people may think of us as heroes. Woe to us if we start to believe that! When we don't find our joy and strength in the Lord, we will be more likely to fall—in fact, it's inevitable.

I have a fairly simple but hopefully effective illustration of this. When I was in high school my friend told me about being locked out of her house. There was no way for her to get in. She prayed and asked God to help her and he did! God answered her prayers and miraculously helped her open the door. I was so impressed by this that I wanted God to do this for me. I wanted a miraculous answer to prayer like that! So I went home and promptly locked myself in the basement. I prayed that God would open the door for me and tried to open it. It didn't open. I prayed again and jiggled the door more forcefully. It didn't even budge. I was so disappointed. Why did God answer her and not me? Just as I was getting ready to try one more time, my mom opened the door and asked me what I was doing. I told her. She said to me, "I don't think God works that way."

Indeed he doesn't. I began to learn then (and continue to learn now!) that life isn't about me and what I want God to do. I guess you would call this philosophy of living where we ask God to see what we are doing and join us in it "Experiencing Me," rather than what Henry Blackaby writes about in *Experiencing God*, where we join God in what he is doing! Life is about God and what he wants to do in and through me. I am not the center of the universe. I cannot manipulate God to do as I please for my joy.

Sometimes my dreams are more about me than God. When we first went overseas I was planning what I wanted to do, how

God would use me, and how others could be impressed with me. However, from day one it didn't go according to my plan at all! As a cross-cultural worker I struggled with the language. I tried to be a good wife and mom in a different culture, and I shared my faith with others, but I had to do so out of weakness. I was not strong. I was not capable. I was forced to depend on God to enable me, which is just the way he likes it! This abiding in the vine and relying on God's strength and not my own is quite biblical! It's just that sometimes, when I was in my home country, life seemed simpler and a facade of deep spirituality could be maintained as long as I was in my comfort zone where it looked like I was able to handle things. Again God brought me to a place where I could continue to learn that life is all about him and his glory . . . not about me. When I am working for my own joy, I cannot find it. However, when my life is about him, it seems that joy and strength are natural (or actually, supernatural!) outcomes.

Life is not about me. It is all about God. I thank him for his patience with me, his constant love, and his continuing work in my life. By his grace, when we forget and fall he catches us, but sometimes we ignore his waiting arms. It is imperative that we, like Nehemiah and his coworkers, look to the Lord for our joy and strength.

Read these words from the song "Joy of the Lord Is My Strength" by Douglas Miller:

> Troubled but not distress
> Makes me not in despair
> For the Joy of the Lord is my strength
>
> Persecuted but not forsaken
> Cast down but I'm not destroyed
> For Joy of the Lord is my strength
>
> Oh, temptation and trials
> I don't worry about
> For the Joy of the Lord is my strength

I'm abused and pushed aside
But I've got the victory
For the Joy of the Lord is my strength

Toward the end of Nehemiah, the people dedicated the walls to the Lord with songs of thanksgiving. They sacrificed to the Lord because he had given them great joy. Their joy was so great that the sound of their rejoicing could be heard from far away.

Nehemiah 12:27,43 says:

> At the dedication of the wall of Jerusalem, the Levites were sought out from where they lived and were brought to Jerusalem to celebrate joyfully the dedication with songs of thanksgiving and with the music of cymbals, harps and lyres . . . And on that day they offered great sacrifices, rejoicing because God had given them great joy. The women and children also rejoiced. The sound of rejoicing in Jerusalem could be heard far away.

When we make God the source of our joy and strength, people will notice. When we were living overseas and I could find very little to read or watch in English, I found a library and began going there about every week. I enjoy reading, but I began to be less discerning about the sexual content of books. As long as the plots were interesting and the story was good, I kept reading, though I felt guilty about some of the things in these books. It seemed like I was losing sight of what holiness was. I felt unclean but trapped by my desire for entertainment. I finally came to the point where I confessed my sin to the Lord and forsook those books at the library. It was a very liberating experience, but not one that I planned on sharing with people.

At a team meeting one of my coworkers was watching me and he soon came up and said, "Sue, it is obvious to me that God has done something special in your life. Will you tell me about it?" He said he saw something in the light of my eyes—I am convinced it was the joy of the Lord. Jesus had once again become my joy and my strength as I had repented of my sin and sought after him. As I confessed my sin and shared about the Lord's forgiveness to this brother, he rejoiced with me at what God had done in my life. I then shared this with others and felt even freer and also more accountable to maintain purity. One thing I learned through this is that when we have secret sins they have power over us. When we confess our sins, God is there, of course, to forgive because of Jesus' work for us on the Cross. But when we also verbally confess our sin to others, that sin loses its hold, its sway, over us. There is no more shame. There is joy in forgiveness that's given by God and affirmed by our brothers and sisters in the Lord.

I invite you to have your own personal feast of booths. Go out into a quiet place under a tree or in a park, and spend some time with the Lord. Evaluate your relationship with him. Have you been ignoring him? Is there an area in which you have been disobedient? Are there any broken relationships that need to be repaired?

Confess these things to God and to a trusted believing friend, but don't continue to grieve. Make this a time of celebration. Revel in his love for you.

You may want to make a timeline of your life over the past four years—what have been the highlights? What have been the lowlights? How have you seen God's faithfulness in each of these? Rejoice in who God is and what he has done for you. Look to him for joy—the joy of life, the joy of your relationship with him, the joy of working for him, and the joy that is yours because of the Holy Spirit in your life.

It is time to rejoice. There is no joy anywhere else. There is no other strength like that which is found in the Lord. We are all weak in and of ourselves. However, the joy of the Lord is our strength. Say it to yourself and personalize it: "The joy of the Lord is my strength."

Live in the joy and strength of the Lord.

Questions:

Are there things you may be feeling guilty about but have yet to repent of? Confess your sins to the Lord and then find a trusted friend with whom you can share your confession.

What is a way for your church to celebrate a "feast of booths"?

Resource:

To understand third culture families and their transitions, go to http://www.interactionintl.org.

Joyfully Persevering
(Habakkuk)

I entitled this chapter "Joyfully Persevering." I dislike even the word "persevering," so it is hard to think of joy as even being in the same sentence. I don't like the time and practice that is involved in enduring toward a goal. After we were married I asked Don to teach me how to play the piano. He said he would be happy to if I would practice for half an hour every day, and he gave me my first lesson. I wanted to sit down and be able to play songs, not just scales or notes. Practice was really boring, so I didn't really give it thirty minutes a day. The next week when it was time for my lesson, I was getting ready but Don wasn't. He said I hadn't practiced enough. I replied that if he didn't live with me he wouldn't know that. "Well," he said, "If I didn't live with you I would charge you money for the lessons!"

And that was the end of my piano career, because I didn't have the tenacity to practice. I wanted to go from knowing nothing to being proficient rather quickly. I saw accomplishment and success as meaning the same thing. They are not necessarily the same.

The person who wrote this well-known parable is unknown, but the author put what I'm trying to communicate into his story. It is the parable of pushing the rock:

> There was a man who was asleep one night in his cabin
> when suddenly his room filled with light and the Savior
> appeared. The Lord told him he had a work for him to do
> and, showing him a large rock, explained that he was to
> push against this rock with all his might. This the man
> did, and for many days he toiled from sunup to sundown;
> his shoulder set squarely against the cold massive surface
> of the rock, pushing with all his might. Each night the

man returned to his cabin sore and worn out, feeling that
his whole day had been spent in vain.

Seeing that the man was showing signs of discouragement, Satan decided to enter the picture, placing thoughts
in the man's mind, such as, "Why kill yourself over this,
you're never going to move it," or "Boy, you've been at it
a long time and you haven't even scratched the surface,"
giving the man the impression that he was an unworthy
servant because he wasn't moving the massive stone.

These thoughts discouraged and disheartened the
man and he started to ease up in his efforts. "Why kill
myself?" he thought. "I'll just put in my time, putting
forth just the minimum of effort and that will be good
enough." And that he did, or at least planned on doing,
until one day he decided to take his troubles to the Lord.
"Lord," he said, "I have labored hard and long in your
service, putting forth all my strength to do that which you
have asked me. Yet, after all this time, I have not even
budged that rock half a millimeter. What is wrong? Why
am I failing?"

To this, the Lord responded compassionately, "My friend
. . . when long ago I asked you to serve me and you accepted, I told you to push against the rock with all your
strength, and that you have done. But never once did I
mention to you that I expected you to move it; at least not
by yourself. Your task was to push. And now you come
to me, your strength spent, thinking you have failed and
ready to quit. But is that really so? Look at yourself. Your
arms are strong and muscled; your back sinewed and
brown. Your hands are calloused from constant pressure
and your legs have become massive and hard. Through
opposition you have grown much and your ability now
far surpasses that which you used to have. Yet still, you
haven't succeeded in moving the rock. Your calling was
to be obedient and to push, and to exercise your faith and

trust in my wisdom . . . and this you have done. I, my
friend, will now move the rock."

God calls us to persevere in obedience. Sometimes this includes
what others would see as success. Other times it includes working
hard and trusting God to do what only he can do when others may
think we are wasting our lives. Obedience and perseverance always
include faith as we persevere in God's call on our lives.

No matter how much I dislike persevering, it is a true and bibli-
cally accurate teaching that joy will come through persevering. Look
at Psalm 126:

A song of ascents.

1 When the Lord restored the fortunes of Zion,
we were like those who dreamed.

2 Our mouths were filled with laughter,
our tongues with songs of joy.
Then it was said among the nations,
"The Lord has done great things for them."

3 The Lord has done great things for us,
and we are filled with joy.

4 Restore our fortunes, Lord,
like streams in the Negev.

5 Those who sow with tears
will reap with songs of joy.

6 Those who go out weeping,
carrying seed to sow,
will return with songs of joy,
carrying sheaves with them.

Verses 1–3 tell us of the great joy the people had as they returned
to their homeland. Verses 4–6 tell us of what is yet to be, reminding
us that after the sorrow comes the joy. They and the nations around
them knew that the Lord was the one who did great things. There
was great rejoicing after a time of intense sorrow. The psalmist is

looking forward to when God would bring all of the captives back, and he uses the picture of sowing and reaping to encourage and comfort himself and his readers.

I did not grow up on a farm. However I have heard about the hard work that farmers do as they plant their crops. Before they plant the crops, they have to prepare the land by removing rocks and tilling the soil. Preparing the ground and planting their seeds is strenuous labor. But in the end, when the corn grows tall and the wheat fields gently wave in the breeze, there is great rejoicing. The hard work is remembered, but with gratitude that the farmers were able to be a part of producing such a wonderful harvest.

Investing in people's lives involves tears. It is impossible to sow without tears, whether we are sowing seed in the lives of family members, friends, or teammates. We never know how people will respond; some people will listen to what we say, and at some point people will disappoint us by not listening.

I remember sharing the gospel with a good friend. She was from a different religious background than me and was not very devout. I knew she understood the gospel when she said, "Do you know what would happen to me if I believed that?" Out of all the people with whom I shared the gospel, she was the one whom I saw as coming closest to believing it. We went home for a summer furlough and when I came back I was looking forward to continuing our conversations. When I saw her, she had changed the way she dressed and had become a more ardent follower of her religion.

I was so discouraged. I was heartbroken. I was sowing in tears. I hope one day to see a harvest and rejoice with songs of joy . . . but some days it is all too easy to see only the tears.

I spent years investing in the lives of my children, seeking to lay a good foundation for them and their faith. There were the normal ups and downs of parenting, and I prayed fervently for each of them. There were times when we made decisions the kids didn't like, and sometimes they made decisions we didn't like! I was asked to referee fights and to determine who started them, though I wasn't there and each blamed the other. I sought to protect my children from harm, but couldn't watch over them 24/7.

As we chat today and my children share more of their experiences, I find out more and more things that cause me to thank God for his watchful care over them. Playing with matches, climbing out windows, tasting battery acid, using machetes, getting sick . . . there were many physical dangers. And as hard as these were, I think they pale in comparison to the broken hearts, doubting faith, and anxious minds. Mothers sow in the lives of the children and they often do so in tears. We often are crying as we pray for them and for ourselves.

Whether we are sowing in the lives of our family or sowing seeds among our unbelieving friends, we will do so with some sorrow and tears. Sowing is hard work. Results may be slow, but if we can continue to walk by faith as the psalmist did, we will return with joy. I know that sometimes it seems like life is all sowing, and that it involves so much work that we cannot see the hope of the future because of the tears of the present.

If we can, like Habakkuk, trust God in the midst of seeming fruitlessness, we can choose to rejoice and be joyful in our God. Habakkuk was seeing injustice unanswered. He was aware of violence and wickedness in the world, and it seemed like God was doing nothing about it.

In *The Bible Knowledge Commentary* on the Old Testament, J. Ronald Blue writes about the message of Habakkuk:

> Though doubts and confusion reign when sin runs rampant, an encounter with God can turn those doubts into devotion and all confusion into confidence. Habakkuk's book begins with an interrogation of God but ends as an intercession to God. Worry is transformed into worship. Fear turns to faith. Terror becomes trust. Hang-ups are resolved with hope. Anguish melts into adoration. (Walvoord and Zuck 1988: 1507)

As Habakkuk saw wickedness prosper and his own people neglect God's law, he questioned God and God answered. God

wanted Habakkuk to look beyond his own nation and into the
world and the events transpiring there. God was aware of what was
happening and completely in charge. Wickedness would not continue to reign. God was going to do something amazing and take
care of everything.

Neither Habakkuk nor we can even begin to understand God's
master plan. We can see only what we can see. There are times when
I am out in my city of 8 million people and can only be overwhelmed
to think that God knows every single person and exactly what is
going to happen to each and every one of them and when. God is
omniscient. He is omnipotent. He is righteous. He is trustworthy.

It is easier to handle the questions of why when we stop
and consider who has the world in the palm of his hands. God
Almighty is absolutely sovereign and in charge of all peoples, all
events everywhere.

We can read Habakkuk's conclusion after becoming more aware
of God's character and power in 3:16–19:

> **16** I heard and my heart pounded,
> my lips quivered at the sound;
> decay crept into my bones,
> and my legs trembled.
> Yet I will wait patiently for the day of calamity
> to come on the nation invading us.
>
> **17** Though the fig tree does not bud
> and there are no grapes on the vines,
> though the olive crop fails
> and the fields produce no food,
> though there are no sheep in the pen
> and no cattle in the stalls,
>
> **18** yet I will rejoice in the Lord,
> I will be joyful in God my Savior.
>
> **19** The Sovereign Lord is my strength;
> he makes my feet like the feet of a deer,
> he enables me to tread on the heights. (NIV 2011)

Circumstances do not cause our joy. Joy does not come because of our hard work or play. We may weep; we may lose everything as Habakkuk alludes to in verse 17. However, we know that as we persevere by faith, joy will come. It may take up just a tiny corner of our hearts in the midst of grief, but as we hang in there it will soon explode inside of us. Circumstances are irrelevant when it comes to choosing joy. Our joy comes because we know God is God and he promises to never leave us and to give us a certain future harvest.

Sowing and reaping, choosing to trust and rejoice in God when everything looks bleak is at the heart of joyful perseverance. Habakkuk made the Lord his joy and strength. In his commentary on verse 18, Matthew Henry wrote of Habakkuk, "He resolves to delight and triumph in God notwithstanding; when all is gone his God is not gone" (http://www.biblegateway.com). We can do the same.

Keep sowing. Persevere. Choose to trust and rejoice in the God of your salvation. As we persevere, we will gain an inner joy and the strength to keep abiding in the Lover of our souls until the harvest comes.

Questions:
In what ways are you sowing while weeping?

How is your church sowing in tears to its surrounding community? Is there a ministry to internationals where more members could get involved?

Resource:
Joy Loewen, *Woman to Woman: Sharing Jesus with a Muslim Friend* (Grand Rapids: Chosen Books, 2010).

Eternal Perspective Brings Joy (Jesus)

At fifty years of age I finished graduate school by writing a three-chapter research paper. Whenever I would turn in my first draft of each chapter, I would wait for its return with the professor's red comments and look at it like I used to watch scary movies: my eyes would be peeking between open fingers in front of my face! I knew there would be a dreadful number of necessary corrections and useful comments. I had to do major rewordings on all the chapters at least three times, as well as several minor and seemingly continual adjustments. A good word to describe the process would be "painful"! However, I kept at it and worked diligently Why? Because I knew the purpose. I knew that in the end I would graduate. I was able to finish well and completed my master's degree.

When I go through difficulties in life, it is often by looking ahead that I endure. When I am at the dentist's office, I know that after a bit of time my teeth will be cleaned or the cavity will be filled. Preparing for a colonoscopy is unpleasant—worse than the colonoscopy itself—but I know that once I have it done, I don't have to do it again for ten years! Studying language brought me closer to the end of language school and the ability to communicate with new friends.

When I get bogged down it is usually because my eyes are only in the present and unable to see anything beyond my current circumstances.

In Romans 12:12 Paul encouraged his readers to "be joyful in hope, patient in affliction, faithful in prayer." First he writes to be joyful in hope. Paul knew that the future is bright for believers.

Even though things might be hard in the here and now, we know our trials are light and momentary compared to the joy and glory that we will experience with Jesus Christ in his future kingdom. Hope involves waiting; joy involves knowing what we are waiting for. This is why Paul could also encourage the Romans to be patient in affliction. The affliction would not last forever. In the same verse he tells them to be faithful in prayer. Prayer is what enables us to be patient and to be joyful through trials as we communicate with our heavenly Father.

Being joyful, patient, and faithful are three needed qualities that will help us when we are going through stressful times in our lives. I remember arriving late at night when we were visiting a city, and our hosts graciously welcomed us into their home. As I sat up the first morning, I looked out of the window to see what their neighborhood was like, since I hadn't been able to see it the night before. There was a large field and a dozen or so men squatting in the distance. It didn't take me long to figure out what they were doing, and I decided that looking out the window wasn't going to be something I wanted to do in the mornings! One afternoon as I was walking into the bedroom to get something, there was only one man squatting in the distance. I started to look away, but he began waving his arm and I didn't know why. As I looked again I saw a wild pig coming toward him. What an awful predicament to be in! What an unusual "back yard view" our friends had and one I was fairly sure I would not want.

However, this family welcomed us into their community. As we walked the streets with them, they pointed out that there were no beggars, as everyone was so poor there was no one from whom to beg! There were small homes with dirt floors and an abundance of flies, annoying monkeys, and barking dogs. During a team meeting, while we were inside the screened windows praying, we saw and heard monkeys loudly screeching while they battled each other for domination of their outside wall.

The hostess was going to bake a dessert and pulled out a big steel box to put over her stove to enable her to use it as her oven.

There was homeschooling to do, visitors coming at all hours, meals to cook, water to heat, a loud generator to fix, and errands to run. She was like the Energizer Bunny and rarely stopped working! Through all of this you could still see her joy. She was where God wanted her to be. It wasn't easy, but she knew the Lord was with her, and her focus was on the eternal, not the temporary challenges.

We joyfully, patiently, faithfully hope to be able to serve through any and all circumstances—not just because they are temporary, but because of the investment we are able to make in eternity. We have a bright future with and for our Savior. Being uncomfortable here on earth is nothing in comparison to that! Though this story is a *very* minor example when compared to those of others who have experienced greater traumas and horrific suffering, this principle is true nonetheless for every trial, no matter how trivial it may seem or how severe. Even the Apostle Paul, with all the persecution and suffering he endured, said that his earthly circumstances were nothing when compared to the glory yet to come.

It is as we look ahead to our secure future with the Lord that we can have joy in what could be a miserable present. Our present is not what we look at to determine how joyous we should be. It is not an indicator of what our attitude should be. We can have joy, no matter what our circumstances, because we know our eternal future is securely promised.

That future hope is what keeps us going when the present is difficult. However, it is not just thinking of the future that gives us hope during present trials, but also looking at the past. Turn to Hebrews 10:32–39 and let's read what the author writes:

> Remember those earlier days after you had received the
> light, when you endured in a great conflict full of suf-
> fering. Sometimes you were publicly exposed to insult
> and persecution; at other times you stood side by side
> with those who were so treated. You suffered along with
> those in prison and joyfully accepted the confiscation of
> your property, because you knew that you yourselves had

better and lasting possessions. So do not throw away your
confidence; it will be richly rewarded.

You need to persevere so that when you have done the
will of God, you will receive what he has promised. For,

"In just a little while,
he who is coming will come
and will not delay."

And,

"But my righteous one will live by faith.
And I take no pleasure
in the one who shrinks back."

But we do not belong to those who shrink back and are
destroyed, but to those who have faith and are saved.

The author is encouraging the Hebrews to look at the past to be
encouraged to have joy for their present. When they first became
believers, they stood their ground in the face of suffering. Whether
they were publicly insulted and persecuted or whether they were
standing by those who were, they stood firm. They sympathized
with those in prison and *joyfully* accepted the confiscation of their
property because they knew that they had better and lasting possessions. They knew their future hope, so they were able to endure their
present circumstances.

As the Hebrews were going through present difficulties, the
author encourages them to look to the past when they had encountered trials and to remember how they had stood firm. They didn't
need to lose heart in the present when they had a rich history of
trusting God joyously through trials in their past. The author exhorts
them to not throw away their confidence but to persevere, looking
ahead to receive what God had promised. In short, they were to keep
walking by faith.

Keeping our faith in the Lord and his goodness, knowing our future is secure with him, we can walk with joy in the midst of suffering.

When I look back, I see God's faithfulness through our two years studying Arabic so that we could communicate the gospel. I see how he worked in and through us, though at times there seemed to be no visible fruit. We longed to see a church of Muslim-background believers planted. We met people, spent time with them, had them in our homes, went to their homes, built friendships with people that we grew to love. We kept praying and sharing the gospel. After about seven years a small cell church was formed as we networked with others and partnered with a local church. We felt that we were flourishing and using our gifts to actually meet with believers and see them growing in their faith! Our kids were happy in their schools; our family was doing well. We rejoiced in God's faithfulness. And then a person in our cell church became an informant and we felt betrayed. Don was told that his work permit would not be renewed and we would need to leave the country. Our kids were devastated. We felt discouraged; just when things were going well, we would have to leave.

The afternoon I found out, I baked a "God's faithfulness" cake. I wanted to do something tangible to encourage myself and my family to remember that God is faithful. I needed to somehow remind us that he was the one closing this door, not the government. And yet, even as I baked that cake, I remember wondering if I would ever be truly happy doing anything else anywhere else again. I was declaring that I would walk by faith: though I wasn't sure what we would be doing, I was going to keep trusting in my Father . . . and I had an inner sense of joy in my God's sovereignty. I knew he had the future under control and that his purpose would not be thwarted.

In the midst of sorrow, I was looking forward with hope and a touch of joy, which is what the author of Hebrews encourages us to do. But God also uses that situation in my life today. When something arises that could shake my faith, I look back and remember God's goodness and faithfulness to us in past times of trial.

The author to the Hebrews encouraged them to not only look at the future and the past to have joy, but also to look to Jesus who set the example of how to go through hardship. He endured the Cross for the joy set before him. He did the will of God. We are to be like him. Read Hebrews 12:2:

> Fixing our eyes on Jesus, the author and perfecter of
> faith, who for the joy set before Him endured the cross,
> despising the shame, and has sat down at the right hand
> of the throne of God. (NASB)

Jesus, the author and perfecter of our faith, endured the Cross because he knew the joy that was waiting for him on the other side. He trusted his Father and knew that, though his present circumstances were dreadful, joy was coming.

When we lose sight of the future and get captivated by what we see in the present, it is easy to lose hope and joy. These two things go hand in hand. Without hope there can be no joy. Let me share with you a true story about a man who lost hope and joy because he was so focused on the present that he forgot about the future God held in his hands. This man lost his eternal perspective. The story is an excerpt from a book by Aggie Hurst, *Aggie: The Inspiring Story of a Girl without a Country*:

> Back in 1921, a missionary couple named David and Svea
> Flood went with their two-year-old son from Sweden to
> the heart of Africa—to what was then called the Belgian
> Congo. They met up with another young Scandinavian
> couple, the Ericksons, and the four of them sought God for
> direction. In those days of much tenderness and devotion
> and sacrifice, they felt led of the Lord to go out from the
> main mission station and take the gospel to a remote area.
>
> This was a huge step of faith. At the village of N'dolera
> they were rebuffed by the chief, who would not let them
> enter his town for fear of alienating the local gods.

The two couples opted to go half a mile up the slope and build their own mud huts.

They prayed for a spiritual breakthrough, but there was none. The only contact with the villagers was a young boy, who was allowed to sell them chickens and eggs twice a week. Svea Flood—a tiny woman of only four feet, eight inches tall—decided that if this was the only African she could talk to, she would try to lead the boy to Jesus. And in fact, she succeeded.

But there were no other encouragements. Meanwhile, malaria continued to strike one member of the little band after another. In time the Ericksons decided they had had enough suffering and left to return to the central mission station. David and Svea Flood remained near N'dolera to go on alone.

Then, of all things, Svea found herself pregnant in the middle of the primitive wilderness. When the time came for her to give birth, the village chief softened enough to allow a midwife to help her. A little girl was born, whom they named Aina.

The delivery, however, was exhausting, and Svea Flood was already weak from bouts of malaria. The birth process was a heavy blow to her stamina. She lasted only another seventeen days.

Inside David Flood, something snapped in that moment. He dug a crude grave, buried his twenty-seven-year-old wife, and then took his children back down the mountain to the mission station. Giving his newborn daughter to the Ericksons, he snarled, "I'm going back to Sweden. I've lost my wife, and I obviously can't take care of this baby. God has ruined my life." With that, he headed for the port, rejecting not only his calling, but God himself.

Within eight months both the Ericksons were stricken with a mysterious malady and died within days of each other. The baby was then turned over to some American missionaries, who adjusted her Swedish name to "Aggie" and eventually brought her back to the United States at age three.

This family loved the little girl and was afraid that if they tried to return to Africa, some legal obstacle might separate her from them. So they decided to stay in their home country and switch from missionary work to pastoral ministry. And that is how Aggie grew up in South Dakota. As a young woman, she attended North Central Bible College in Minneapolis. There she met and married a young man named Dewey Hurst.

Years passed. The Hursts enjoyed a fruitful ministry. Aggie gave birth first to a daughter, then a son. In time her husband became president of a Christian college in the Seattle area, and Aggie was intrigued to find so much Scandinavian heritage there.

One day a Swedish religious magazine appeared in her mailbox. She had no idea who had sent it, and of course she couldn't read the words. But as she turned the pages, all of a sudden a photo stopped her cold. There in a primitive setting was a grave with a white cross—and on the cross were the words SVEA FLOOD.

Aggie jumped in her car and went straight to a college faculty member who, she knew, could translate the article. "What does this say?" she demanded.

The instructor summarized the story: It was about missionaries who had come to N'dolera long ago . . . the birth of a white baby . . . the death of the young mother . . . the one little African boy who had been led to Christ . . . and how, after the whites had all left, the boy had grown up and finally persuaded the chief to let him build a school in the village. The article said that gradually he won all his students to Christ . . . the children led their parents to

Christ . . . even the chief had become a Christian. Today there were six hundred Christian believers in that one village . . .

All because of the sacrifice of David and Svea Flood.

For the Hursts' twenty-fifth wedding anniversary, the college presented them with the gift of a vacation to Sweden. There Aggie sought to find her real father. An old man now, David Flood had remarried, fathered four more children, and generally dissipated his life with alcohol. He had recently suffered a stroke. Still bitter, he had one rule in his family: "Never mention the name of God—because God took everything from me."

After an emotional reunion with her half-brothers and half-sister, Aggie brought up the subject of seeing her father. The others hesitated. "You can talk to him," they replied, "even though he's very ill now. But you need to know that whenever he hears the name of God, he flies into a rage."

Aggie was not to be deterred. She walked into the squalid apartment, with liquor bottles everywhere, and approached the seventy-three-year-old man lying in a rumpled bed.

"Papa?" she said tentatively.

He turned and began to cry. "Aina," he said, "I never meant to give you away."

"It's all right Papa," she replied, taking him gently in her arms. "God took care of me."

The man instantly stiffened. The tears stopped.

"God forgot all of us. Our lives have been like this because of him." He turned his face back to the wall.

Aggie stroked his face and then continued, undaunted.

"Papa, I've got a little story to tell you, and it's a true one. You didn't go to Africa in vain. Mama didn't die in vain. The little boy you won to the Lord grew up to win that whole village to Jesus Christ. The one seed you planted just kept growing and growing. Today there are six hundred African people serving the Lord because you were faithful to the call of God in your life . . .

"Papa, Jesus loves you. He has never hated you."

The old man turned back to look into his daughter's eyes. His body relaxed. He began to talk. And by the end of the afternoon, he had come back to the God he had resented for so many decades.

Over the next few days, father and daughter enjoyed warm moments together. Aggie and her husband soon had to return to America—and within a few weeks, David Flood had gone into eternity.

A few years later, the Hursts were attending a high-level evangelism conference in London, England, where a report was given from the nation of Zaire (the former Belgian Congo). The superintendent of the national church, representing some 110,000 baptized believers, spoke eloquently of the gospel's spread in his nation. Aggie could not help going to ask him afterward if he had ever heard of David and Svea Flood.

"Yes, madam," the man replied in French, his words then being translated into English. "It was Svea Flood who led me to Jesus Christ. I was the boy who brought food to your parents before you were born. In fact, to this day your mother's grave and her memory are honored by all of us."

He embraced her in a long, sobbing hug. Then he continued, "You must come to Africa to see, because your mother is the most famous person in our history."

In time that is exactly what Aggie Hurst and her husband
did. They were welcomed by cheering throngs of villagers. She even met the man who had been hired by
her father many years before to carry her back down the
mountain in a hammock-cradle.

The most dramatic moment, of course, was when the
pastor escorted Aggie to see her mother's white cross
for herself. She knelt in the soil to pray and give thanks.
Later that day, in the church, the pastor read from John
12:24: "I tell you the truth, unless a kernel of wheat falls
to the ground and dies, it remains only a single seed. But
if it dies, it produces many seeds." He then followed with
Psalm 126:5: "Those who sow in tears will reap with
songs of joy." (Hurst 1986).

Be joyful in hope. Be patient in affliction. Be faithful in prayer.
Amen.

Questions:
Describe how you have experienced God's faithfulness in the past,
and tell how that encourages you as you face today.

How many people in your congregation know the history of your
church? Give an update on the history of cross-cultural ministries
with which the church has been and is involved.

Resource:
Ralph D. Winter and Steven C. Hawthorne, eds., *Perspectives on the
World Christian Movement: A Reader*, 4th ed. (Pasadena: William
Carey Library, 2009).

Joy in the Midst
of Suffering
(the Macedonians)

During troubling times I'm not sure I even want to read what James tells us in chapter 1:2–4, "Consider it all joy, my brethren, when you encounter various trials, knowing that the testing of your faith produces endurance. And let endurance have its perfect result, so that you may be perfect and complete, lacking in nothing" (NASB).

However, it is true. It is a joy to grow in grace. I can see that my faith grew as I learned endurance and I became more mature in my walk with God. My faith before living overseas seems a bit shallow to me now. When going through hardship with no comforts of home, faith must grow and endurance is a result. After time I was able to encourage newcomers to rejoice . . . that though they would face trials and hardship, God would use it in their lives and in the lives of those who observe them.

God has always used people who go through hardship with joy to encourage others facing trials. Turn to 1 Thessalonians. Thessalonica was located at the intersection of two major Roman roads, one leading from Italy eastward and the other from the Danube to the Aegean. Thessalonica's location and use as a port made it a prominent city. It became the capital and was a major port of the entire Roman province of Macedonia.

Read what Paul writes to the Thessalonians in 1 Thessalonians 1:6–10:

> You became imitators of us and of the Lord, for you welcomed the message in the midst of severe suffering with

the joy given by the Holy Spirit. And so you became a model to all the believers in Macedonia and Achaia. The Lord's message rang out from you not only in Macedonia and Achaia—your faith in God has become known everywhere. Therefore we do not need to say anything about it, for they themselves report what kind of reception you gave us. They tell how you turned to God from idols to serve the living and true God, and to wait for his Son from heaven, whom he raised from the dead—Jesus, who rescues us from the coming wrath.

First of all, we see that the Thessalonians became imitators of Paul and of the Lord in that even though they suffered, they did what was right. They welcomed the message with joy given by the Holy Spirit. Galatians 5 mentions that joy is a fruit of the Spirit, so we know that true joy comes from him. As the Thessalonians followed Christ in spite of suffering, they became a model to all the believers in Macedonia and Achaia, and as a result the message rang out throughout all of these two regions, both of which made up the country of Greece. Everyone knew what had happened in Thessalonica. News spread as people talked about them in light of chapter 1 verse 3: their work of faith (how they turned from idols to worship God), their labor of love (how they served the living God), and their hope in our Lord Jesus Christ (how they were waiting for him to come back).

As the Thessalonians followed Christ, regardless of suffering, I'm not sure they realized the extent of their influence on the world around them. We don't always realize our influence either. There may be times you are feeling discouraged because you are not seeing immediate or visible results from your ministry.

Years ago our organization had workers in Iran. Several of the men went to a nearby village to preach the gospel and never had any noticeable response. Fast forward about thirty years when one of the men who had served there receives an email from a man from that village. It turns out he and his family are followers of Christ. Not only them but several others in that village came to faith, and there is a small house church meeting. The fruit of their labor was unknown for thirty years.

You may be feeling discouraged because you don't see how God is at work through you, using your spiritual gifts. You don't sense that you are making a difference. You may wish you had spiritual gifts that are different from the ones you have.

It reminds me of the relationship I see between spiritual gifts and chocolate. Let me explain. I met Don during my second year of college and we began dating. Sometimes I would go to the store and see candy bars. I would buy one for me and one for Don. I would eat mine and plan to give the other one to Don so that he would know I was thinking about him. However, if I didn't see him right away, the candy bar would start looking better and better to me as the day wore on, and I would end up eating it. Later, when I saw Don, I would tell him I bought him a candy bar. His eyes would light up until I told him I ate it. After this happened several times, he finally told me that he would prefer not knowing I bought him a candy bar if I was going to eat it and not give it to him. I bought it for him and really meant to give the gift to him, but I ended up keeping it as I began thinking and acting like it was really for me.

At times in my life I have looked at spiritual gifts like I did those candy bars. God gave me spiritual gifts to benefit others, but it is easy to think the gifts were given to me for me. It can also be tempting to base my significance on what my spiritual gifts are. If I think my gifts are useful or important, I feel good about myself. If I see others with the spiritual gifts I wish I had or that I feel are more important than mine, I can feel insignificant in comparison.

I remember wanting to be a single, traveling youth evangelist. It didn't really matter to me that I didn't have the gift of singleness or evangelism—it would have been a significant ministry. When I was sharing my faith overseas as a married woman and not seeing anyone come to know the Lord and I heard of those who were seeing fruit, my second reaction was joy. My initial gut reaction was envy.

I wanted to be able to do that! I didn't feel that my gifts were that important and I wanted the gifts I didn't have.

God continues to teach me that we were given the spiritual gifts he wants us to have so that the church can work together to bring honor to him, not to make us feel either significant or insignificant. Rather than feel envious, I practice thanking God when I see others using their spiritual gifts. Rather than feel jealous when I hear of someone leading a seatmate on the plane to the Lord, I can praise God and not feel resentful—even when I remember the time when I prayed for an opportunity to witness on a train and sat next to a woman who left to find another seat as soon as the train started!

I wasted too much time when we were first overseas feeling guilty that I didn't have the spiritual gifts I thought I should have had and feeling discontent with the gifts I did have. I thank God that we, as believers, need each other. The Lord has gifted each of us so that as we use our gifts and work together, Jesus is the one who is honored.

As we use the gifts God has chosen to give us, we must recognize that we influence others when we don't even realize it, just like the Thessalonians did. Remember in 1 Thessalonians 1:7, Paul stated that the Thessalonians were a model to believers in Macedonia. Now we find Paul mentioning the Macedonians as models to encourage the Corinthians in 2 Corinthians 8:1–5:

> And now, brothers and sisters, we want you to know about the grace that God has given the Macedonian churches. In the midst of a very severe trial, their overflowing joy and their extreme poverty welled up in rich generosity. For I testify that they gave as much as they were able, and even beyond their ability. Entirely on their own, they urgently pleaded with us for the privilege of sharing in this service to the Lord's people. And they exceeded our expectations: They gave themselves first of all to the Lord, and then by the will of God also to us.

The Thessalonians had been role models for the Macedonians, and we see the Macedonians growing and serving God faithfully themselves. Now Paul is using the Macedonians as examples for the Corinthians. He mentions them not only here, but also in 11:9: "And when I was with you and needed something, I was not a burden to anyone, for the brothers who came from Macedonia supplied what I needed" (NASB). Paul also mentions them and their generosity to the Romans in Romans 15:26, 27:

> For Macedonia and Achaia have been pleased to make a contribution for the poor among the saints in Jerusalem. Yes, they were pleased to do so, and they are indebted to them. For if the Gentiles have shared in their spiritual things, they are indebted to minister to them also in material things. (NASB)

Whenever I hear of someone giving so generously, I almost always assume they are fairly wealthy and able to give much. However, the Macedonians gave in the midst of (notice these adjectives) a *severe* trial and *extreme* poverty . . . but notice also they gave from their *overflowing* joy. They urgently pleaded for the privilege of sharing to minister to others. They went out of their way to give. Even though they were in dire circumstances, their joy was overflowing and they wanted, indeed they felt compelled, to share generously and richly.

How do severe trials, extreme poverty, and overflowing joy add up to rich generosity? I think the secret is in the latter part of verse 5: They gave themselves first to the Lord and then to others in keeping with God's will. They sought to be in God's will by giving themselves first to him.

I do not like the acronym JOY—Jesus, others, and you—or the philosophy, "God first, family second, and ministry third." How does one do that? How does a person know when she is putting Jesus first? If a person is always putting others before herself and there are no boundaries, I can see burnout looming in her future. Why is family so often listed separately from ministry? Is how I serve

my family not true ministry? Trying to make life fit a nice formula
to make it seem simple just doesn't work, because life isn't simple.
Ministry isn't simple. How I invest my time can be complicated. I
like what Paul says better—let's give ourselves first to the Lord and
let everything else flow from that.

When we give ourselves first to the Lord, we find our source of
joy. We then give ourselves to others who will be influenced by that
joy. As we have seen with the Macedonians, none of this is dependent
on our circumstances. It is dependent on our relationship with God.

There have been times I was terrified of the will of God. What if
it was sorrow and not joy? My husband's dad was forty-six when he
died of a heart attack. I didn't think much about it when we married
at twenty-one years of age and as we started out our life together
as husband and wife. We were young, healthy, and excited about
serving God together.

The years went by and before I knew it we were in our forties.
One night in July of 1999 we received a phone call telling us that
Don's brother went home to be with the Lord. Larry had seen the
doctor in May, and it looked like he was in good shape and that his
diet and exercise were effective in maintaining a healthy heart. Two
months later he was dead at forty-nine from a fatal heart attack.

Don wanted to talk about life insurance. I said that I didn't
want to talk about it. He wanted to discuss funerals, and I refused.
As he pursued issues related to death or dying in our conversation,
I wanted to change the topic. One night as we were lying in bed
and I was upset that he again wanted to talk about life insurance, I
turned a deaf ear. He became aware of how upset I was and asked
me what he could do or say to help me. I told him that I wanted him
to promise me that he was not going to die anytime soon and that
we would grow old together and die around the same time. He said,
"I can't say that." I burst into tears as I replied, "I know. That's the
problem."

During that time I found that I was so afraid of what could
happen and so focused on what might be that I was failing to enjoy

the present. It didn't seem to matter that my husband was healthy and we were together right then. I was worried about what might happen in the future. Eventually the Holy Spirit convicted me of my lack of faith, contentment, and obedience to what Jesus taught in Matthew 6:25–34:

> Therefore I tell you, do not worry about your life, what you will eat or drink; or about your body, what you will wear. Is not life more than food, and the body more than clothes? . . . Can any one of you by worrying add a single hour to your life? . . . But seek first his kingdom and his righteousness, and all these things will be given to you as well. Therefore do not worry about tomorrow, for tomorrow will worry about itself. Each day has enough trouble of its own.

As I repented and chose to not only thank God for today but to give myself to him today, I was ready to seek his kingdom first and not worry or be anxious about tomorrow. I found myself able to talk with Don quite calmly about life insurance, funeral plans, and burial places. I was learning (and am continuing to learn) to find my ultimate security in God, not in another person or stable health.

It was thrilling to me when we made it past our forties and turned fifty. We are both on a low-fat, low-cholesterol diet. When our son came home from college for break and tasted a few of these meals on our new diet plan, he said, "If you want me to move out, just tell me!" Don exercises faithfully and I am exercising more than I used to. We do our best to take care of ourselves so that we can grow old and continue to serve God together.

There is no guarantee for tomorrow except for knowing that God holds it securely in his hands. There is no assurance for health except for knowing that God works everything together for our good and his glory. Our body parts have no warranty except for the promise of a new, glorified body in the future.

When I thought about it, God's word had given me great security for the future and all the guarantee I will ever need! I didn't have to worry about the future; I could trust God for today as well as tomorrow. I discovered though that when I gave myself and my loved ones to him, I could trust him to do what was best. He gave me peace and joy in my heart. I realized anew that we all belong to God and that he can give joy even when life is hard.

As we follow after God, we can know that whether we see it or not, whether it is tomorrow or forty years from now, we are influencing others. You may be the first person to share the gospel with another person, somewhere in the middle, or maybe the one to lead her to Christ. Your faith in God during a difficult time may influence others to trust God more. How you respond to a hurtful comment may challenge others to turn the other cheek. Know that God is using you for his glory as you seek after him. The message of God is going out. You can rejoice in knowing God is at work.

Before we give ourselves to anything else, we must first give ourselves to the Lord. When we do that, our joy and poverty, even in the midst of trials, will well up into rich generosity as we are then able to give to others.

Questions:
Who are some role models in your life for whom you are thankful to God? Write a thank-you note to someone who has influenced you and let them know how God has used him or her in your life.

How can the church minister to the parents of cross-cultural workers?

Resources:
Cheryl Savageau and Diane Stortz, *Parents of Missionaries: How to Thrive and Stay Connected When Your Children and Grandchildren Serve Cross-culturally* (Colorado Springs: Authentic, 2008). And the website http://www.pomnet.org is especially for parents of cross-cultural workers.

V
Transitions, Travel, and Tiredness

The longer we've been in cross-cultural ministry, the more we have traveled. I remember before we left for our first term we were at a family reunion in Tennessee. At that point in time, several of my uncles had served in the military overseas, but I don't think anyone else in the family had a passport.

My grandpa was sitting outside with his cousin and, as I walked by, my grandpa said, "This is my granddaughter Susan." His cousin was a man of few words and he simply replied, "Yep." My grandpa continued, "She and her family are going overseas." Again came the standard reply, "Yep." Clarifying further, my grandpa added, "They are going to share the gospel." Then his cousin said, "Why else would they go?" He could think of no other reason good enough for leaving the U.S.!

I thought leaving the first time would be the hardest. I was wrong. Each time we go back and each time we return, it never is easier. Saying good-bye to family, to children, and now to grandchildren is a heartrending farewell each time! As children marry and grandchildren come, there are just more people to love and more people to miss! I remember being so happy when we heard that a new grandbaby was coming and then crying in the car as we left, grieving that I would not be there for him as much as I would like. As our parents get older it becomes more difficult to say good-bye to them as well.

In one airport there was a bomb threat that closed the hall that would take us from where we were to the terminal where we needed to be to catch our flight. Don made me (can you sense an attitude problem in me?) run outside through the cold in a less-than-direct route to the terminal so we wouldn't miss our flight. Never mind that the bomb might have been where we were running! We had tightly spaced connections and I remember racing through airports trying to catch the next flight while trying to catch my breath at the same time! I remember trying to locate a pharmacy in an airport that sold something to help the diarrhea I was trying to cure before getting on a plane for a long flight! There have been lines so long we couldn't find the end and officials so slow that it seemed to take forever just to get through security. At one airport the bathroom was so filthy that I had a hard time believing I was at an international airport, because it reminded me of the outhouse at my cousin's farm!

We've had things taken away and, by a few acts of kindness, we were able to keep what we shouldn't have had! In one Middle Eastern airport the official found a small pair of scissors in my husband's bag. He said they had to go. Don said they were the best pair he ever had, and the man let him keep them. I don't think that would have ever happened in America with a Middle Eastern man with scissors and an American official!

Through travels alone or with small kids and big ones, good food and bad, God has watched over us. He has given peace in the midst of turmoil and grace to say all the good-byes and hellos that come with the job description of a cross-cultural worker.

Once he even protected me from getting on the wrong plane! Although I wonder where it was going . . .

Trains, Planes, and Automobiles

When I think about all the firsts I've experienced since beginning cross-cultural work, I feel tired. Just looking back at the different modes of transportation we've taken is exhausting!

I've been on big planes and little planes. Most planes I've been on have landed normally, but there was one that did a spiral landing. There were plane rides that lasted up to seventeen hours. Traveling with four small kids has its own set of challenges, even on shorter flights! To help travel go more smoothly, I would get each child his or her own backpack stuffed with things for their enjoyment and entertainment. When the boys were younger, I put in a couple of squirt guns. (What was I thinking?) Anyway, as the backpacks went through security, one of the guards asked me if they had toy guns. When I said yes, he told me that they don't allow play guns on the airplane since they could be mistaken as real ones. I was a bit confused but said he was free to take them out. When he pulled out two little lime-green and neon-pink plastic squirt guns, he sheepishly gave them back to us and said, "They looked more real in the image on the screen. You can keep them."

I've done a lot of walking along the sidewalk or streets with various animals. There were always the normal cats and dogs that, though battered and bruised, managed to roam the streets. But there were also water buffalo, camels, goats, sheep, chickens, cows, and even an elephant along the way! Even in cars I wasn't completely separate from the animals, like the time a water buffalo's tail swished my face through the open window of a taxi!

I've been in taxis where I could see the road below my feet and in one where the door would fly open whenever we went around a turn! There have been nice taxis with air conditioning and not-so-nice taxis that broke down under the hot sun in 105-degree weather!

I rode in my first bicycle rickshaw in the heat of the day and marveled at the strength of the driver. I also rode in an auto rickshaw. One auto rickshaw we were in died on its way up a bridge. Another auto rickshaw driver pulled up behind us, stuck his foot on the bumper of our auto, and pushed us up and over the bridge as his engine propelled both vehicles forward!

I'd ridden on a motorcycle with my husband. I even tried to ride one by myself, though I only succeeded in popping wheelies . . . about eight in a row, which could be impressive if that was what I was trying to do! I was simply trying to go forward. Once, there were three of us on a motorcycle: the driver, Don in the middle, and me hanging on tightly from the back!

I've been on boats that didn't look sturdy enough to make it down the river and back. Some were sailboats, others were motorboats, and yet others were rowboats. I've seen a dead cow floating by our boat on the Nile and, in the distance, dead bodies being burned on the Ghats of the Ganges.

I rode an overnight train along with my husband, and when I went to use the restroom I saw the train tracks through the open floor below the toilet. When it was almost time to go to sleep, I realized we had a traveling companion. I first saw the mouse peeking at us from the floor of the train when we were making our seats into beds. "Do mice climb?" I asked my husband. He assured me they didn't. But when I asked him if he was telling me the truth or simply what I wanted to hear, he merely smiled. I had heard stories of thieves on the trains who steal your things. We had what was recommended to prevent that: our suitcases were locked into position with bicycle locks. Once I lay down, I had my purse strap wrapped around my arm and my other bag wound securely around my ankles. I would wake up with different turns or stops of the train and peek underneath the bed to make sure our suitcases were still there!

As I think back and see God's faithfulness no matter how many different ways we've traveled to wherever we were going, I still wonder . . .

Do mice climb?

Questions:

How has God assured you of his presence in the midst of your travels?

What are some of the challenges that cross-cultural workers experience in their travel?

Resource:

Bill Richards and E. Ashley Steel, *Family on the Loose: The Art of Traveling with Kids* (Bellevue, WA: Rumble Books, 2012).

Reentry Challenges!

We were back in the U.S. for our home assignment. The boys were eight and six years old. The girls were four and two. We were coming through customs, and the officer asked a few questions to see if the information we gave would match the information he had in our passports.

He asked our oldest son, "When were you born?"

Misunderstanding the question, my son proudly answered, "Dallas, Texas." Hmm. My youngest daughter, though it was her first time in America, calmly and confidently tried to walk by him as he continued to ask questions of our family. After assuring him we had enough money to live on and showing him our checkbook, we were allowed to enter our country. It wasn't quite the welcome we had expected.

My parents met us at the airport and took us out to eat where they offered ice cream for dessert. Our kids were so excited! When the waitress asked what kind of ice cream the kids wanted, one said, "*Karkaday*" ("hibiscus" in English). Another child said, "I want mango!" Baffled, the waitress said they didn't have either of those. My kids wondered what kind of ice cream place didn't have such normal flavors!

After some time adjusting to the U.S., we wanted to have the kids checked out by a doctor to make sure they were doing well and made an appointment to have them all seen in one afternoon. The nurse came into the examination room and gave each of the boys a cup. She looked at them and said, "Urinate in the cup." To our defense, please note we still had a two-year-old and so we had never really gotten around to upgrading our terms for bodily functions.

We still used "pee-pee" and "poopie" or, in general, just "potty."
When I was little I remember using terms like going "number one"
and "number two." We hadn't even gotten to the numbering terms yet!

So it was no wonder my sons were confused. Stephen asked,
"I'm a what in the cup?"

The nurse, looking a little perplexed, stressed each syllable of
the unfamiliar word, "No. I said ur-in-ate in the cup."

My younger son looked up and asked, "What am I, a six in the cup?"

Eventually communication occurred, the boys learned a new
vocabulary word, and everyone got checked out by the doctor and
was pronounced healthy!

I guess we could have gone out for ice cream to celebrate, but
selection of flavors was so limited!

Questions:

How can we prepare ourselves and our children for reentry
challenges?

How can churches better understand the changes and challenges that
cross-cultural workers encounter?

Resources:

Lois A. Dodds and Lawrence E. Dodds, *Am I Still Me? Changing
the Core Self to Fit a New Cultural Context* (Liverpool, PA:
Heartstream Resources), http://www.heartstreamresources.org/
media/AMISTILL.pdf.

The Scarred Purse

I was riding on the Madrid metro recently feeling pretty savvy. The last time I had been on it with Don, someone stole his backpack. So I had my hand on my suitcase, and my purse was tucked securely under my arm. As I got off the train and we sat to wait for the next one, my friend looked at my purse and said, "Sue, you've been sliced. What did they take?"

I looked down and saw a long gash in my fairly new purse. Thankfully it had two layers. The outer layer had a huge gash and the inner layer had a shorter gash. I had just put in a bottle of water and a bag of pretzels, and where he cut was where they were resting. (There is something to be said for carrying snacks!) Way over on the other side of my purse was my wallet, and the passport was in a different pocket altogether. As I got back to the hotel I looked through my things and, as far as I could tell, nothing was stolen.

But I still had a long flight to get back home, and my holey purse wouldn't travel well. I was able to get a needle and thread from the hotel and sew up both layers of the purse with three different colors of thread. It had a smaller scar on the inside which no one could see and a much larger and more colorful scar on the outside which everyone could see! It held together and I made it safely back home.

As I looked at the ugly scar on my recently purchased purse, I felt angry at the thief. Then I almost (not quite) felt sorry for the one who tried to steal from me but was unable to reach anything, except for an unwanted bottle of water and bag of pretzels. Now, after some reflection, when I look at the scar I am not just reminded of attempted robbery; I am also reminded of God's good hand of protection. Sometimes he protects us through something; other times he protects us from something. I don't know how he chooses which to do, but either way, we know he is always good and his grace is always sufficient.

I was going to throw it out and get a new purse right away, but I hung onto it for a while. It may be scarred, but it had a story to tell. I guess it's kind of like me!

Questions:

How has God used a "scar" in your life to be a blessing as you shared your story with another person?

What are ways you can encourage cross-cultural workers as they deal with difficult challenges?

Resource:

The Christian Hospitality Network offers free getaways for cross-cultural workers: http://www.christianhospitalitynetwork.com/about/missionary_getaways.

Change?

Transitions. Changes. Alterations. Shifts. Modifications. Adaptations. Amendments. Transformations . . . There are a lot of different words for what we all go through as cross-cultural workers.

As someone going through many changes myself, I need all the encouragement I can get. Don and I had been in our new host country three weeks. We saw a "spit bin" but felt no inclination to use it. We walked among cows on the street. We lost electricity and ran out of water. We went sightseeing and shopping. I learned how to make chai, eat spicier foods, and take an afternoon rest. Staying hydrated and escaping mosquitoes are two challenges. Having had someone cook our lunches is nice and would be easy to get used to! I feel lonely at times; I miss our grandchildren. And after finally learning my way around my previous hometown, I am starting over in a new place.

One night when the electricity was off and the mosquitoes were on, I wondered if being here was a good idea. And then I had to smile. The next week I was going to speak at a women's conference, and one of my topics was perseverance. God was giving me an opportunity to practice what I would preach. I chuckled a bit at the irony and, though I didn't sleep any better, my attitude improved as I thanked God for the lesson. The next morning I told Don about this opportunity I had to put into practice what I was going to speak about. Since he was dealing with the same issues, he said that he didn't think that he should have to be included in lessons meant for me!

Change is seldom easy for less adventurous people like me. However, it does have its advantages. I realize anew I cannot and indeed should not trust in my own strength and wisdom. Change drives me to rest in and cling to the Lord and not to rely on my own strength or understanding. Change makes me run to my never-changing refuge, my rock, and find him faithful yet again. It challenges me to think through my priorities and rediscover what is really important and lasting. There is a new spirit of adventure and an opportunity to explore new horizons.

So for me change is hard but good, kind of like going to the dentist or that yearly visit to the gynecologist. I can dislike it, but I do it because I know it is better for me in the long run.

So now that I think about it . . . I may have changed my mind. I like change.

Unless I change my mind again!

Questions:
How does the fact that God never changes affect you when you are going through changes?

What do you think are some of the major changes cross-cultural workers experience when they first go overseas?

Resource:
Marjory F. Foyle, *Honourably Wounded: Stress among Christian Workers*, rev. ed. (Grand Rapids: Kregel, 2001).

Blessed Are the Aged

I can't remember if this happened before or after one of the boys asked about the year I was born: "You were born in 18-what?" Regardless, my daughter once asked me why my hair was turning white. I told her it was a symbol of maturity and wisdom. She said, "Oh, I thought you were just getting old!" It wasn't long after that I started coloring my hair to cover up the grays that were becoming more and more prevalent. That same daughter recently asked me when I was going to stop coloring my hair. I asked her why she was asking, and she replied that she had found some gray hairs and didn't want to be grayer than her mother! I remember when I was younger that I said I would never color my hair, that I would age gracefully and be proud of my age. Well I am proud of my age, and I am aging still hanging on to that amazing grace, so I guess that counts as aging gracefully!

There is something to be said for aging. As we get older, we know more than we used to, and people ask us for advice and look to us to know more about life. For the most part, I don't mind getting older. I try to take care of myself. I eat healthier than I did when I was younger (though maybe too much chocolate) and exercise regularly (which doesn't seem to help due to the chocolate!). I am getting used to being one of the older women. It does seem a little unsettling to hear people talking about history and realize that, since I was alive during much of what they are talking about, I never really considered it history!

The first time someone came to me and said she wanted to talk to an older woman, I couldn't figure out why she was telling me that. Then I realized. Oh, *I* am the older woman. At first it was weird.

I don't feel old. As I have gotten even older, I kind of like being an older woman and I find myself embracing this new status.

Being reminded that I am older even shows up when I'm having my devotional time. I remember reading Psalm 71 and really enjoying it and finding it meaningful. Then I read the subtitle (this is manmade and not inspired, praise God) of it being a "psalm for the aged."

People used to say I looked too young to be a grandma. No one says that anymore. One of the ways I know I am getting older is by how waitresses and salespeople treat me. "What can I get for you, young lady?" As soon as someone calls you a young lady, you know you are either very young or very old. For the very young it is supposed to make them feel more grown up. For the very old it is supposed to make you feel much younger. For me, it makes me feel old, because if they are trying so hard to make me feel young, I must be old. My friend who is in her seventies says that when she shares insights at a Bible study they tell her she is cute. She told me that means they think she is old, but they want to encourage her. I know when I hit that stage of being "cute" that I will think of her and recognize yet another step in the aging process.

The only time I have felt young in recent years was when I taught a Sunday school class for women. I loved that class. Everyone in it was older than me and I never called any of them cute! I was too busy learning from them—probably more than I ever taught them.

At the end of class, when I walked out the door, I would hear the phrase, "See you next week, kiddo."

When I look back at that, I think, "She was so cute!

Questions:

How does your view of aging differ from the views of your home and host cultures?

How does your culture's view of the elderly differ from some of the countries where cross-cultural workers serve?

Resource:

T. J. Addington, *Live Like You Mean It: The 10 Crucial Questions that Will Help You Clarify Your Purpose / Live Intentionally / Make the Most of the Rest of Your Life* (Colorado Springs: NavPress, 2010).

Three's a Crowd!

We arrived at the airport and stood in line for an hour. There was no one at the ticket counter. We waited and found out our flight was cancelled. We then learned that the airline would put us up in a hotel room and rebook us for a flight the next day. After waiting in line three more hours, we finally were able to get to a bus that would take us to the hotel.

It was February 13. I thought this wouldn't be all bad. It was almost Valentine's Day. The hotel was being paid for by the airline. Dinner was provided. It would be a free date, time for us to spend with each other sandwiched in between busy weeks of ministry. I had four hours in line to dream, and I began to like the idea—I was looking forward to our free gift of a romantic evening for Valentine's Day! Waiting in line wasn't too much to pay for a little getaway!

We were waiting in yet another line at the hotel when we found out that they were putting three to a room. They introduced us to Carol who would be rooming with us. We had asked if we could pay extra to have a private room, but the hotel clerk said they were full. Before heading to our room we asked the desk what time the shuttle would take us to the airport. He said it hadn't been determined yet. As the three of us went out for coffee and had dinner together, we enjoyed getting to know each other, but it wasn't quite what I expected our romantic Valentine's Day hotel stay to be like! We all decided to go to sleep early. Carol was in the far bed. I was in the next bed. Don was on the cot nearest the door. We still didn't know what time we were supposed to leave in the morning.

Around 10:30 p.m. there was a knock at the door. Don went to open it. "Room check," the man called. Nothing else was said. I asked

Don what that was all about, but he didn't know. We went back to sleep, but another knock came at the door at 2:30 a.m. The man asked what time our flight was. Don gave him our flight information but did not learn anything about the time of our departure from the hotel. At 4:30 a.m. Carol went downstairs to see what time her shuttle would leave. Hers was leaving right away, and she told us ours would leave at 6:00 a.m. We said good-bye to our roommate and slept a little more before we got up to get ready to leave.

As Don and I were telling friends about what happened, I was explaining that it wasn't as romantic as I expected it to be since we were never alone. Don observed that we did have that hour alone together after Carol left. "But," I reminded him, "we didn't know when the next room check would be!"

Questions:

What are traveling tips you have found helpful when delays and cancellations occur?

When can you invite a cross-cultural worker out for coffee and ask to hear some of their stories? Discover ways to help care for cross-cultural workers while they are near your church.

Resource:

Charles A. Warner, *Caring for Missionaries on HMA-Furlough*, version 4.0 (Rockford, IL: Barnabas International, 2011), http://www.barnabas.org/files/Caring%20for%20Missionaries%20on%20HMA-Furlough--19%20February%202011--version%204.0.pdf.

Minor Inconveniences Can Add Up to a Major Headache

It isn't really one thing that makes me want to go home; it is an accumulation of a lot of little things . . .

First there is the electricity or lack thereof. True, it was kind of fun playing Scrabble by candlelight. It wasn't as much fun trying to do a load of laundry with both a lack of water and a lack of electricity. One day it took nine hours—let me repeat that . . . NINE HOURS—to do one load of laundry. I could have flown to Paris and gotten a chocolate croissant in the time it took to do that one load of laundry!

One night I had an important conference call and there was a brownout. There was some electricity but not enough to get the Internet to work. As long as there was some electricity, the inverter wouldn't kick in and provide enough electricity for the Internet to work. My husband is a genius. He turned off the electricity so we could use the inverter and have enough electricity to make the conference call. It's just weird . . . turning off electricity to get electricity.

I think I mentioned the lack of water in my nine-hour load of laundry, right? I learned that you can take a bath and wash your hair with a bucket half-full of water and a smaller cup to dip it out with. I can think of nothing harder than running out of water. Without water you can't do dishes, get a drink, wash clothes, or flush the toilet. Conservation is key when using the water you do have.

I feel nervous in traffic where white lines don't really mean anything. There can be three lanes in theory, but in reality there are six or more. You can turn in any direction from any lane, and cars turn their lights on only in intersections at night. Buses, cars, bikes, motorcycles, trucks, and cows all vie for position on the roads, and whoever is even a nose ahead of the others has the right of way. Unless you are a cow—then you have the right of way all of the time!

Loneliness feels heavy. I miss family and friends, and it just takes time to meet people. There are language barriers and, even when the language being spoken is English, it doesn't necessarily mean you can understand it or be understood.

Finding stores and learning what is available and what isn't are challenges. I recently found a bag of Cheetos with Chester the Cat on the familiar orange bag, but when I opened them they were spicy. They weren't what I was expecting. Some days it seems that everything here is spicy. The spring rolls at the Chinese restaurant and potato chips can all be spicy and burn my mouth.

I was even nervous when I opened up a package of Chips Ahoy cookies that I found. I was bracing myself in case they were spicy too.

Water, electricity, traffic, loneliness, shopping, and eating . . . none of them are a big deal on their own, but when you need to cope with them all at one time it can feel overwhelming.

In some cases it can also produce a headache. When that happens, it is easy to fix. Just eat a spicy snack and your mouth is so hot you don't even think about your head anymore! You're just hoping there's enough water to drink to cool off your tongue!

Questions:

What have been the hardest things you have had to adjust to in your new culture?

Recognizing that cross-cultural workers go through difficulties you can't relate to, what are some difficulties you go through to which they can't relate?

Resource:

Peter Jordan, *Re-entry: Making the Transition from Missions to Life at Home* (Seattle: YWAM Publishing, 1992).

A Walk Like No Other

I should have known the city we were going to visit was a bit backward, as that is how our train pulled into its station. We went to visit coworkers. They were so kind to us and worked hard to make us feel welcome. Don had eaten something on the train (probably not a good idea) and wasn't feeling well. I guess that is putting it mildly since he told me he was feeling so sick that he told God that if he wanted to take him to heaven, it would be fine with him! Thankfully he started feeling better, and we invited our host family out to dinner. We wanted to do something nice for them before leaving their town. They said there was a hotel with not only a restaurant but also air conditioning! By the time everyone was ready to go it was dark.

"Did you bring your flashlights?" they asked. Don and I looked at each other and replied that we didn't think to bring them. They didn't think that would be a problem as they had several, and so we started off. Five adults and four children left their house and began the long walk to the restaurant.

Did I mention it was the end of monsoon season? The streets were extremely muddy, and in order to navigate the streets people strategically put in bricks or rocks to act as stepping-stones through the mud. With flashlights held high we tried to find them. We also learned that cell phones can cast enough light to help us find the best path.

Sometimes there were no rocks, but there was a slim outer curb where we could walk, trying to maintain our balance as we made our way. At one point I lost my balance and one foot slid into the slime.

Step. Slosh. Step. Slosh. Oh well, the restaurant wasn't too much further.

However, we came to a place where there were no rocks (or maybe they were submerged) or outer curb. So we climbed up to walk on top of the walls surrounding the streets to go around the mud. Up and down, some walls were higher and others were lower, as we continued our trek to the restaurant and air conditioning.

At one point there were no walls to climb up on. There were no bricks to guide our steps. There was, however, a slight brick edge around a building. Facing the wall and clinging to it, we made our way, step by step, in single file around it. We made it around that wall, and as we began to step on bricks again we saw several wild pigs on the same path just ahead of us.

As they meandered away I began to relax more until I heard one of the kids say, "The worst is just ahead!" I had to laugh, but I was a bit worried as well! What would be worse? I asked him what he meant, and he said he just meant it would be harder for the smaller children. The adults wouldn't have a problem. Good—I was an adult.

We soon walked past a public sink (at least it appeared to be a public sink since it was there in an alley for anyone to use) with a faucet that worked and pipes that were broken beneath the tub. So, as one person washed his feet in the sink above, I put my one slimy foot underneath the sink and rinsed it off as water poured out of the broken pipes. I arrived at the restaurant with a clean, but wet, foot!

We sat, talked, and enjoyed a lovely meal together.

And then it was time to return home. Flashlights and cell phones held high, we began the trek back.

Questions:

What helps you stay positive in the midst of challenging circumstances?

Have a little fun with your family. Turn off all the lights in the early evening and pretend there is no electricity for one hour or two if you are adventurous. No computers, no TV, no Internet access. Use only flashlights or candles. Afterwards, discuss what would help people who face this more consistently to stay positive and not give in to complaining when facing challenging circumstances.

Resource:

David James, *Sixteen Seasons: Stories from a Missionary Family in Tajikistan* (Pasadena: William Carey Library, 2011).

Lesson Learned from the Camel Market

There's nothing like having family come to visit you in your host country. They get to see where you live and work. It eases some of their fears and gives them a better idea of what you do.

Don's mom and two of his brothers came for a visit. He went to meet them at the airport, and when his mom saw him she burst into tears. He thought it was because she was so happy to see him. We found out later it was because he had lost so much weight she thought he looked unhealthy!

They came to our apartment and played with our kids. They went to church with us, met our friends, and saw some of the local sights that every tourist sees. We ventured to the pyramids, rode a sailboat on the Nile, shopped at the *souk*, and explored fascinating museums.

As "locals" we also knew some places off the beaten track that we thought they would enjoy experiencing, and thus we invited them to the camel market. On the edge of the city away from modernity and anything urban, we walked through the crowds of buyers, sellers, and a few other gawkers. We saw hobbling camels, bleating goats, doomed sheep, and one beautiful black stallion—all for sale. The stallion did not want to be hooked up to pull a dinky wagon and was letting everyone know it was beneath him. Rearing up, he defied those seeking to tame him. Purchased camels were being loaded into a Toyota pickup truck. It was a fascinating process to watch these proud creatures prodded and goaded into a sitting position with a big stick and sturdy rope. Hit, pull, hit, pull . . . several men worked until two subdued and slightly stunned camels were sitting side by side in the back of the small truck bed.

Through the market, items were for sale. You could buy ropes, iron tools, camel accessories, crafts, chickens, food, and drinks. I guess you could say it was similar to a bustling county fair. In one corner of the market was a village woman stirring a huge black cauldron of bubbling bean stew over an open fire with the biggest wooden spoon I have ever seen. Several of us were watching her, and others were looking at the animals.

One brother saw it happen. The woman at the cauldron blew her nose into her fingers and then tossed what came out into the air. At that exact moment the second brother saw something land in his mother's hair. Not knowing what it was, he used his hand to remove it. A little boy (observant little fellow) gave a tissue to the second brother as he tried to help his mom and clean off his hand! Before long, both brothers were trying to help their mother, albeit laughing as they did so. Don's mother wasn't sure what was in her hair, but she knew it was not good. She soon realized the truth as the brother who had seen it all explained what had happened.

You can imagine the range of reactions. There was surprise, shock, and an overall feeling that can best be stated as "yuck," resulting in uproarious laughter. The more we thought about it, the more we laughed. It wasn't long after that we headed home—we had seen all we wanted to see and touched more than we wanted to touch. I'm not sure Don's mom was laughing as much as the rest of us, but she showed great resilience and lightheartedness as what she did next will testify.

She went immediately to the bathroom to wash her hair . . . several times to make sure it was totally clean. She soon came out with a towel still wrapped around her hair and jokingly observed, "Now I know why women here wear veils!"

Questions:

How have you adjusted the way you dress to fit into your new culture?

Women cross-cultural workers often have to dress very conservatively in the cultures where they work. How do you define and practice modesty in your culture?

Resource:

Christine A. Mallouhi, *Miniskirts, Mothers, and Muslims: A Christian Woman in a Muslim Land* (Grand Rapids: Monarch Books, 2004).

VI
A Deeper Look at
Faith, Love, and Hope

I was meeting with a young woman who was considering cross-cultural ministry. She was counting the costs and asked me about the sense of rootlessness that might come with the territory. How does her heart's longing for a home, a place of her very own, fit in if God is calling her to serve him overseas?

I told her the good news and bad news. The good news being that cross-cultural workers catch the idea that this world is not our home. From the time we experience life in a different culture and realize we don't really fit there—but neither do we fit in our home culture any longer—we recognize that heaven is where our eternal citizenship is and where we truly belong. The bad news is that life can be uncomfortable in a world that is not our home. Constant hellos and good-byes fill our lives as those who work across cultures; changing homes and switching countries and assignments (due to our choice or to factors out of our control) become normal.

Sometimes when we go to our home country and see people our age with their own homes and family living nearby, jealousy creeps into my heart and a longing for roots envelops me before I know it. It takes a while to work through those feelings of envy and to come to God again and affirm that his calling is my privilege and that my heavenly home is enough. I am not cheated. I will not be resentful. It is a wonderful opportunity to trust God for our home here while I wait for my heavenly one.

Really, we all trust God for our homes. He just provides in different ways for different folks. It's not like I am living by faith and everyone who owns a home isn't. All believers walk by faith, trusting in God to provide for us. He is the owner of all things and provides for all peoples. It's just that believers recognize where all that we have comes from and that all that is here will one day disappear. Believers know we need to lay our treasures up in heaven.

That is true security. No thieves, no fires . . . nothing can take that inheritance away. Our home is in heaven. Here on earth we may own or rent our homes, but in reality they all belong to God!

Now that is what I consider to be deeply rooted! It doesn't matter where our family roots are here as long as our eternal roots are firmly established in our Lord and Savior. In order for the roots to be healthy, we all need three main ingredients: faith, love, and hope. Let's take a deeper look at these three things.

Work Produced by Faith Includes Joy and Suffering

We were rejoicing by faith, though we were sad that we had to leave the country we called home for eight years. We moved from that country to another host country for several years but eventually returned back to our home country for about twelve years. As we began praying about moving again to a totally different part of the world, I would have almost rather stayed in our home country than move again. But we desired to follow God's will for our lives and felt that he was leading us to move. So we did. We moved halfway around the world and now use our new home in South Asia as a base from which to serve and to travel.

We travel quite a bit in our roles, so we are always coming and going, even from our new home. Once we had been gone for about six weeks when we arrived back in our host city early one Friday morning. Our flight landed around 4:30 a.m., and it was around 7 a.m. when we got to our apartment. We went inside and found the electricity had been cut off, the Internet was disconnected, termites were sawing away at our bed and at a shelf, a horde of ants was attacking a pile of insect eggs in a drawer, rain had come into the kitchen, the water heater was leaking, and a tire on the car was almost flat. It was almost enough to make me want to go back to the airport and get back on the plane to go anywhere else as long as it had electricity! I remembered our calling, gave thanks for a safe trip, and laid down to rest before tackling anything!

You can't be in ministry long without seeing and probably experiencing suffering and heartache. While suffering differs in its intensity and frequency, truth is always truth when dealing with it. Whether a friend is martyred, a church plant falls apart, you are betrayed by a colleague, or your home church has dropped your support, God is always near and lets us know how to respond. Scripture tells us to rejoice always, to recognize that Jesus spoke truly when he said in John 16:33, "In this world you will have trouble. But take heart! I have overcome the world." (NIV 2011)

Often in Scripture we see joy and suffering together in the same context. How can that be? Have you ever noticed how the Christian life includes two seemingly contradictory things that somehow work together? We try to comprehend free will and the sovereignty of God and we know that both are true, but how? We hear Jesus saying that to live we must die, to gain we must lose, to be first we must be last, to be great we must serve. There are some paradoxes like these that we have to grapple with as believers.

Turn to 1 Thessalonians. In a previous chapter we looked at a very brief history of the city; now let me share with you a little background on how the Thessalonian church—the recipient of two of Paul's letters—began.

We can read about how the church started on Paul's trip to Thessalonica in Acts 17. He and Silas had previously been imprisoned in Philippi. They had been preaching the gospel and delivered a slave girl from demon possession. Since the owners could no longer make a profit from this girl's fortune-telling abilities because of what Paul had done, the owners brought them to court and had them beaten and arrested. There was an earthquake and, having been delivered from prison and leading the jailer to the Lord, they then met with believers in Philippi to encourage them. Paul talks about this in 1 Thessalonians 2:2: "We had previously suffered and been treated outrageously in Philippi, as you know, but with the help of our God we dared to tell you his gospel in the face of strong opposition."

After leaving Philippi they went to Thessalonica, and here we know they continued to preach the gospel in the synagogues and some people believed. But others were jealous and formed a mob to start a riot. Paul wrote about it in 3:4: "In fact, when we were with you, we kept telling you that we would be persecuted. And it turned out that way, as you well know."

When the rioters couldn't find Paul and Silas to arrest them, they pulled out Jason and some other brothers to take to the city council, where they were forced to post bond in order to leave. That night the brothers sent Paul and Silas away to a different city. Paul makes reference to this in 2:17: "But, brothers and sisters, when we were orphaned by being separated from you for a short time (in person, not in thought), out of our intense longing we made every effort to see you."

Paul had made a strategic choice by going to Thessalonica when he left Philippi. This city was uniquely stationed to be used as a center for the spread of the gospel to the whole Balkan Peninsula. It was a seaport and linked sea and land routes to the interior of Macedonia. In Paul's choice, we see his desire was to see the gospel spread around the world.

Indeed, as we'll see later, the church at Thessalonica was critical in the spread of the gospel. Right now, though, let's look specifically at 1 Thessalonians 1:2,3: "We always thank God for all of you and continually mention you in our prayers. We remember before our God and Father your work produced by faith, your labor prompted by love, and your endurance inspired by hope in our Lord Jesus Christ."

In these next three sections we are going to look at these things—faith, love, and hope—and discover that each involves two apparently contradictory things that God somehow uses together to grow us in our faith and to spread the gospel for his glory:
1. Work produced by faith includes joy and suffering.
2. Labor prompted by love involves transformation and sacrifice.
3. Endurance inspired by hope entails working and waiting.

Let's begin with looking at work produced by faith.

Do you remember when your work of faith began? Mine began when as a youngster I heard about Jesus. I tried to be good. I think I wanted to please God. I behaved in school and got good grades. I tried to be kind to others. But I felt like I was lacking . . . something. I looked at others and they always seemed more talented, more beautiful, and more confident. As I went to church I believed in God and Jesus. But as a young teen I was asked to pray one Wednesday night, and I realized I didn't really know how to talk with God. Around that same time my younger cousin asked me why I wasn't a Christian. I told him I was, but in my heart I knew I wasn't. I was trying to save myself and depending on the wrong things to get me to heaven.

It wasn't long after my cousin's question that a special speaker came to our church and shared the gospel. God was at work and that night I believed. I had faith that God in Christ had forgiven me for my sins and that which was lacking was now filled. That night my life was forever changed; a work produced by faith had begun. I remember going to junior high school the next morning full of joy and finding my best friend, Debbie. I went up to her and said, "Debbie, I got saved last night!" She grabbed my arm, pulled me to the side of the hallway, and said, "Shhh! I'm saved, too, but we don't have to talk about it!"

I remember being very confused. How could I not talk about it? One of the most joyous things in the world had happened to me, most of which I didn't even understand at the time—I didn't know that I had been transferred from the kingdom of darkness into the kingdom of light; I was once not a people but now belonged to God; I was once his enemy and now I was his friend; I was once an alien and now I was a part of God's family; I was once without mercy and destined for wrath. In that one moment of work produced by faith I was forever destined to share in his glory. I only knew my sins were forgiven and that I was loved by God. It was something I had to share with others.

I think I know what her main concern was and why she didn't want to talk about it. Think back to junior high. Did you enjoy junior high? I'm pretty sure that when people are asked if they could relive any time in their lives that junior high would not be a common response! Everyone wants to fit in. We tried to dress alike, think alike, and be like others so that we wouldn't stick out in the crowd. Why is that? It is because we didn't want to be seen as different, because if we were different we might be ridiculed and left out of the group, and in junior high that feels like persecution!

As an adult, and as I have seen and heard about severe persecution of brothers and sisters around the world, I recognize that anything I might have experienced in junior high and high school as I took a stand for Christ is not what I would call persecution today. But it felt like it then, and the resources I needed then are the same resources that the Thessalonians needed when they faced persecution.

Let's take a deeper look at what this work of faith is.

The Greek word for "work" is *ergon*, meaning an undertaking, employment, business, or work. Their undertaking or work was one that was produced by faith.

Faith (*pistis* in Greek) is a conviction of truth, a belief; faith is to trust in God. Paul writes that they believed it; they welcomed the message with joy given by the Holy Spirit in spite of suffering.

So we see that this work of faith involves joy and suffering. Isn't it strange that these two things are mentioned in the same context? Joy comes from the Holy Spirit, and suffering has no effect on the joy that comes from him. They could have joy in spite of the suffering they experienced.

The Thessalonians' work produced by faith began with their recognition that idols could not save them. Paul elaborates on this in verse 9 when he says that they turned to God from idols. The believers in this city were comprised of Jewish converts, God-fearing Greeks, and a number of prominent women. It would appear that many of the believers were Gentiles who came out of idolatry. At that time the Thessalonians had separate gods for everything: gods of war and love, earth and sea, pleasure and anger, heaven and hell. The ancient Greek religion, adopted by the Romans, was willing to add gods, but they didn't want to subtract any. Yet when they came to Christ, the Thessalonians rejected all their former gods. Why? It is because this was a work that was produced by faith—faith in the one true God. They realized that nothing else could save them. Only God could, because of what Jesus Christ had done for them on a cross.

A true work produced by faith leaves all idols behind and trusts in God alone. This not only happens at salvation, but the Holy Spirit continues to convict us when we start looking elsewhere for security or loving something else more than the Lord. We start walking by faith and we continue walking by faith.

Paul writes that it was this work of faith that began in the Thessalonians that caused the gospel to spread. Read with me in 1:4–10:

> For we know, brothers and sisters loved by God, that he has chosen you, because our gospel came to you not simply with words but also with power, with the Holy Spirit and deep conviction. You know how we lived among you for your sake. You became imitators of us and of the Lord, for you welcomed the message in the midst of severe suffering with the joy given by the Holy Spirit. And so you became a model to all the believers in Macedonia and Achaia. The Lord's message rang out from you not only in Macedonia and Achaia—your faith in God has become known everywhere. Therefore we do not need to say anything about it, for they themselves report what kind of reception you gave us. They tell how you turned to God from idols to serve the living and true God, and to wait for his Son from heaven, whom he raised from the dead—Jesus, who rescues us from the coming wrath.

Because the Thessalonians came to faith and continued to walk by faith, they soon became a model to others, and the Lord's message rang out not only in surrounding areas but everywhere! Why was their influence so great? Please notice with me verse 6: "You welcomed the message in the midst of severe suffering with the joy given by the Holy Spirit."

A true work of faith seems to always include these two elements: suffering and joy. How is it that these two things go together?

They seem miles apart in their meanings, and yet they are found together in Scripture.

I think we hear a lot about Christ, salvation, and joy in the West. Everyone seems to have heard that God loves us and has a wonderful plan for our lives. We know that we have our home in heaven, and there is great joy as God provides for our needs. People may come to Christ to receive joy, to have a happier life, to know of a home for them in heaven, and to escape the fire of hell. I think I came to the Lord for selfish reasons. I didn't want to go to hell. I needed my sins to be forgiven. Jesus paid the price for my sins and was giving me a gift. I liked that and came to know him. But I was very "me" centered. Many times when I shared the gospel with my friends, I would focus on a "happier" or more fulfilled life on earth and forevermore. It's all true to a point, but I needed to learn more about denying myself, taking up my cross, and following him.

Where there is only a focus on joy, people are unprepared for trials and may fall away from the faith. Paul had been concerned for the Thessalonians as he knew they were experiencing persecution. He knew they had joy, but how would they do when they were tested? What would happen to them? Could they stand firm? He sent Timothy to check on them and was greatly encouraged when he heard from Timothy that they were indeed standing firm. This is one reason that the message rang out from them so clearly—they stood firm. It wasn't just about the joy they experienced. It was also the suffering they endured. Their work of faith, though tested, was found to be secure and strong.

One thing we don't hear a lot of sermons about in North America is suffering. As a matter of fact, I heard a pastor pass right over the concept of sharing in the sufferings of Christ onto sharing in his glory when preaching from Romans 8:17. One of our highest values as North Americans is comfort. No one likes to think about suffering or talk about it, and surely no one wants to experience it. I think this lack of teaching on and preparation for suffering is one of the major reasons we can be ill-equipped to live and serve cross-culturally.

We've been trained by our culture to want the joy he gives us and to avoid the suffering to which he has called us.

It is not wrong to have joy, to revel in the love God has for us and to be thankful for our eternal heavenly home. However, to be true to the meaning of joy and the meaning of suffering, I wonder if we can really have one without the other. My expectations of being a cross-cultural worker and of God were laced with a lot of joy. I expected blessing since I was choosing to serve the Lord wherever he sent me. I didn't spend much time thinking about suffering. I'm not alone in this.

Robynn, in *Expectations and Burnout,* writes about what she expected of God in ministry and what she grew to understand about suffering:

> I know now that my expectations of God were faulty. I didn't expect a rose garden, but neither did I expect that the disappointments and the pains would be so relentless, so incessant, so continuous. I didn't look for a life that would eventually be written up in hard-backed biography, but I did sort of expect a little bit of success, a little bit of visible fruit. I looked for God to rescue me and release me from the hurt of it all. And that's not how God works. I know that now. God *is* strange and weird. His ways *are* perplexing and hard pressing. He's in this for His glory. Somehow mysteriously we get to be a part of that. We get to watch. And His glory *will* shine! Stand back. See the bigger picture. There is a story of redemption and grace at work all around us. In the messiness of the details He is there . . . deeply devoted to us, deeply at work in us—redeeming and gracing us, too. But all of that happens best in the space of suffering. I didn't expect that. I wasn't looking for that. (Eenigenburg and Bliss 2010: 153)

It is as we suffer and as we experience joy that the world realizes we are no longer a part of it like we used to be. When these two things—joy and suffering—are evident in our lives, one result is that the message of the gospel will spread.

We have to recognize that the joy that Paul is writing about is not self-induced. It is given by the Holy Spirit. Joy is a fruit of the Spirit. It is not feeling happy all of the time. When suffering comes we don't simply smile and act as if it doesn't hurt. No, this joy is deeper. It actually abides through the pain. This joy is impossible apart from the power of the Holy Spirit. And we can have it in spite of suffering as we look to him as the source of our joy.

How is it possible to experience joy in the midst of suffering?

Let's look in other scriptures to discover where joy and suffering are linked together and what we need to know in order to experience joy in the midst of suffering.

Look at Acts 5:41. There Luke records that after being flogged, "the apostles left the Sanhedrin, rejoicing because they had been counted worthy of suffering disgrace for the Name." The apostles could rejoice because they considered the worthiness of his name worth the suffering they endured. His worthiness counted more than their comfort. Joy is mine when I recognize that the treasure I have in the Lord is far more valuable than anything I can hold onto in this life.

In John 12:27,28 Jesus is talking about his impending death. He said, "Now my soul is troubled, and what shall I say? 'Father, save me from this hour'? No, it was for this very reason I came to this hour. Father, glorify your name!" Jesus knew he was going to suffer, but he also knew that he had come into the world for just this purpose. So he refocuses on glorifying God as his main goal in life and in death. We too can follow Jesus' example and not always ask to be excused from suffering, but ask God to glorify his name through it. When I am in the midst of a difficult situation and am tempted to ask to be saved from it, I need to remember Jesus. I must recognize that it is possible God brought me to "this hour" so that I could glorify his name through it rather than escape from it. In my humanness I almost always look for escape. It is only with eyes of faith that I can remember why I am living and that though his purpose includes me, it is bigger than me.

Paul also connects joy and suffering in Romans 5:1–5 as he looks at the results of suffering:

> Therefore, since we have been justified through faith, we have peace with God through our Lord Jesus Christ, through whom we have gained access by faith into this grace in which we now stand. And we boast in the hope of the glory of God. Not only so, but we also glory in our sufferings, because we know that suffering produces perseverance; perseverance, character; and character, hope. And hope does not put us to shame, because God's love has been poured out into our hearts through the Holy Spirit, who has been given us. (NIV 2011)

Not only do we consider the worthiness of God through our sufferings, but we rejoice in the hope of the glory he alone deserves and will get as we endure by faith. We also recognize in the midst of our suffering that God not only gets glory, he is at work in us for our good.

That is why in Romans chapter 5, Paul goes on to say that we can rejoice in our sufferings because we know that our suffering will ultimately bring about good things. Suffering brings about perseverance. Perseverance produces character. Character results in hope.

When we suffer we learn to persevere, to last, to endure by trusting God. When there is no escape and we just have to go through something difficult, we see God's faithfulness and experience his grace; we learn that we can do this—by God's grace we can persevere! We know God was with us in the past and he gives us hope for the future.

We see how God supplies, how he works, how he comes through for us. We learn to trust him especially when he doesn't do what we want when we want! We know he has a plan. We learn more about who he is and who we are, and we develop into people of hope. We

see beyond our present difficulties into the future of what God might
be doing in and through us and our situations.

So we see that suffering produces good things in our lives and
can rejoice as we grow in perseverance, maturity, character, hope,
and a growing awareness of the love of God.

Let's look also at what Peter writes in 1 Peter 4:12–16:

> Dear friends, do not be surprised at the fiery ordeal that
> has come on you to test you, as though something strange
> were happening to you. But rejoice inasmuch as you
> participate in the sufferings of Christ, so that you may be
> overjoyed when his glory is revealed. If you are insulted
> because of the name of Christ, you are blessed, for the
> Spirit of glory and of God rests on you. If you suffer, it
> should not be as a murderer or thief or any other kind of
> criminal, or even as a meddler. However, if you suffer as
> a Christian, do not be ashamed, but praise God that you
> bear that name. (NIV 2011)

Did you notice the contrast between rejoicing that you can
participate in the sufferings of Christ and being overjoyed when his
glory is revealed? The glory will far outweigh any sufferings we
may be presently enduring. I have often prayed for a mistreated and
seemingly forgotten brother rotting away in an Egyptian prison, that
he would see just a glimpse of the glory of God in the midst of his
pain. He will one day see that all that he has endured for his Lord
will result in great glory for his Lord. The suffering will pale in
comparison.

We have the joy of knowing Jesus, recognizing his worthiness,
desiring his glory, and understanding the good work that God does
in our lives in the process of suffering. We also must grasp the truth
Peter is talking about: we can rejoice when we participate in the sufferings of Christ. I'm not sure I understand fully what that means,
but I recognize that it is a privilege we have. He suffered for me, and
now I can participate in that by suffering for him. We can rejoice
now for the suffering and even more so when his glory is revealed.

I find these truths to be very helpful in the midst of suffering. What is also helpful is keeping in mind that the work produced by faith that Paul talks about involves the work of God as well as our own work.

In 1 Thessalonians 2:13 Paul writes, "And we also thank God continually because, when you received the word of God, which you heard from us, you accepted it not as a human word, but as it actually is, the word of God, which is indeed at work in you who believe." The word of God works in us. Remember Romans 10:17? "Faith comes from hearing, and hearing by the word of Christ" (NASB). As we spend time meditating on the truths of Scripture, God himself works in us and he uses his word in our lives.

At the same time that God's word is at work in us, we also work and work hard. Again, this is another paradox. It seems incongruous that these can happen at the same time. Yet we read in Philippians 2:12,13:

> Therefore, my dear friends, as you have always obeyed—
> not only in my presence, but now much more in my
> absence—continue to work out your salvation with fear
> and trembling, for it is God who works in you to will and
> to act in order to fulfill his good purpose.

In times of trouble I have felt like I was the one doing all the work: all the effort to persevere, to keep growing, to keep living was all being done by me. It is only when I look back that I can see the grace of God and how it was his hand that pulled me through.

Think back to when you first felt called to cross-cultural ministry. Why do you do what you do? What is it that makes sane, reasonable women in one culture leave it to go to another? We leave our way of life, our families, and our friends to live in a new place, learn a new language and culture, to make new friends and often new families. We probably make less money than we could have. We might not be as comfortable as we could be. Why? What made you leave the known for the unknown, an easier lifestyle for a more difficult one?

Isn't the motivation a work produced by faith, a work in which God and you are both involved? You realized that idols could not save you, so you turned to God and the work produced by faith began. You were born again. Your walk of faith began. And as you serve him wherever you are, the work produced by faith continues as you walk by that same faith experiencing joy and suffering.

There are times when the road is bumpy and suffering seems to be our constant companion while joy is a long-lost friend. If we're not careful we can lose sight of eternity and our faith falters. When that happens, we can be tempted to do work produced not by faith but by fear. There can be fear of people. What will other people think if we admit we are tired? What will happen to our reputation if others know we are struggling? What would others say if we told them we felt like giving up and going back home?

We can also be afraid of God. What if he isn't pleased with our service? We can ask why he isn't doing more in and through us. We may feel pressure to have more tangible results because of guilt, peer pressure, or pride. Work produced by fear, or any of these things stemming from fear, is work from the wrong motivation.

None of these motivations will bring us joy . . . only emptiness, selfishness, and anxiety. With those kinds of motivations we are tempted to put on an act of self-sufficiency that ends up depleting our soul of any delight at all. The message doesn't spread. Others aren't influenced. Eventually we give up, burn out, or stop caring. Faith gives way to despair and hope is lost.

We must remember that we are not people of fear. We are not driven by pride or guilt. We are women of faith, and this work produced by faith in our lives involves both suffering and joy.

As we continue to walk by faith, we see that God is at work in and through this work of faith. And like the Thessalonians, the message will ring out through us. Our lives will influence those around us and those we don't even know personally. Remember, this is a work produced by faith . . . faith in Jesus Christ. This is beautifully pictured in the following story:

The Road of Life

At first, I saw God as my observer, my judge, keeping
track of the things I did wrong, so as to know whether I
merited heaven or hell when I die. He was out there sort
of like a president. I recognized His picture when I saw it,
but I really didn't know Him.

But later on when I met Christ, it seemed as though life
was rather like a bike ride, but it was a tandem bike, and I
noticed that Christ was in the back helping me pedal.

I don't know just when it was that He suggested we
change places, but life has not been the same since. When
I had control, I knew the way. It was rather boring, but
predictable . . . It was the shortest distance between two
points. But when He took the lead, He knew delightful long cuts, up mountains, and through rocky places
at breakneck speeds, it was all I could do to hang on!
Even though it looked like madness, He said, "Pedal!"
I worried and was anxious and asked, "Where are you
taking me?" He laughed and didn't answer, and I started
to learn to trust.

I forgot my boring life and entered into the adventure.
And when I'd say, "I'm scared," He'd lean back and touch
my hand. He took me to people with gifts that I needed,
gifts of healing, acceptance and joy. They gave me gifts
to take on my journey, my Lord's and mine.

And we were off again. He said, "Give the gifts away;
they're extra baggage, too much weight." So I did, to the
people we met, and I found that in giving I received, and
still our burden was light.

I did not trust Him, at first, in control of my life. I thought
He'd wreck it; but He knows bike secrets, knows how to
make it bend to take sharp corners, knows how to jump
to clear high rocks, knows how to fly to shorten scary
passages. And I am learning to shut up and pedal in the

strangest places, and I'm beginning to enjoy the view and
the cool breeze on my face with my delightful constant
companion, Jesus Christ. And when I'm sure I just
can't do anymore, He just smiles and says . . . "Pedal."
(Anonymous)

Questions:
What are the differences between the characteristics of a woman of
faith and a woman of fear?

What are symptoms of living in fear and not by faith? What can be
done to help?

Resource:
MaryAnn Cate and Karol Downey, *From Fear to Faith: Muslim and
Christian Women* (Pasadena: William Carey Library, 2003).

Labor Prompted by Love Involves Transformation and Sacrifice

In the last chapter we looked at 1 Thessalonians 1:2, 3 where Paul wrote, "We always thank God for all of you and continually mention you in our prayers. We remember before our God and Father your work produced by faith, your labor prompted by love, and your endurance inspired by hope in our Lord Jesus Christ." We focused on the work produced by faith. Now we are going to take notice of the labor prompted by love and how it involves transformation and sacrifice.

It is too easy to think that we can sacrifice easily. We can choose what we want to give up and do so. I gave up our house. Though difficult at the time, it now seems easy compared to some of the things I have been called on to give up since then. Our choices of what to give up are usually augmented by God as he works in us, empowering us to sacrifice what he knows we must in order to grow in our faith in him and love for others. When we give up what is hard to give up, transformation can take place. When my husband was diagnosed with a possible cancerous tumor, I did not want to give him up and entrust him to God. I pleaded for healing, but also came to the point when I knew I had to entrust him to the Lord. By God's grace we committed him and his tumor to the Lord. Of course we are thankful it was benign, but we also know God's grace is always sufficient no matter what the outcome would have been.

We would not have chosen to leave our first country of service, and felt especially hurt that it was due in part to a spy whom we thought was a trusted friend in our cell church. God chose to shut that door and to transform us as he taught us about forgiveness and trust in the midst of sacrifice and moved us to a different place for ministry.

As I walked through those trials, I realize that I didn't often think much about the transformation that needed to take place in my own life so that I could learn to labor in love. Maybe I thought I didn't need it. Couldn't I just serve without having to go through painful transformation? If I thought I could sacrifice only what I chose to, what were my motives? Did I desire to serve God out of love for him or because of a desire to be used by him, possibly even to get some glory for myself by how much I sacrifice for him? What does this labor prompted by love look like, and how do transformation and sacrifice fit in?

At first glance you might think that the words "work" (like the "work of faith" we looked at in the previous chapter) and "labor" (this "labor of love" that we are going to look at now) are similar. They are not. This word "labor" is the Greek word *kopou*, and it means intense labor, a beating of the breast, sorrow, troubles. This is harder than work and implies intensity in the labor and in the pain we feel as we toil.

You would be right if you thought that the love mentioned here is *agape* love, that godly love which is unconditional. I think it would have to be this unconditional kind of love that would prompt someone to labor and strive through sorrow and troubles.

Paul goes on to describe in verse 9 what their labor prompted by love looked like. Remember he wrote that they turned from idols (that was their work produced by faith) to serve the living and true God. This service to God is their labor of love.

We already discovered from this passage that they suffered and experienced persecution, and Paul was worried about them. Persecution wasn't new. He even mentions that they had become imitators of the churches in Judea as he wrote in 2:14–16:

> For you, brothers and sisters, became imitators of
> God's churches in Judea, which are in Christ Jesus: You

> suffered from your own people the same things those
> churches suffered from the Jews who killed the Lord
> Jesus and the prophets and also drove us out. They dis-
> please God and are hostile to everyone in their effort to
> keep us from speaking to the Gentiles so that they may
> be saved. In this way they always heap up their sins to the
> limit. The wrath of God has come upon them at last.

Their own countrymen had turned against them just as had happened in the churches in Judea. Paul wondered about them as they were undergoing such hardship. He had warned them persecution would come. How were they doing as they faced opposition? Remember, we previously read that Paul was so concerned he sent Timothy to check on them, and he was delighted to learn from Timothy on his return that the Thessalonians were standing firm in the Lord in the midst of sacrifice. Paul had been praying and was greatly encouraged that they were not only standing firm in the Lord, they were living to please God. This is what he says in 3:6–9:

> But Timothy has just now come to us from you and has
> brought good news about your faith and love. He has
> told us that you always have pleasant memories of us and
> that you long to see us, just as we also long to see you.
> Therefore, brothers and sisters, in all our distress and
> persecution we were encouraged about you because of
> your faith. For now we really live, since you are standing
> firm in the Lord. How can we thank God enough for you
> in return for all the joy we have in the presence of our
> God because of you?

Then he goes on to say in 4:1, "As for other matters, brothers and sisters, we instructed you how to live in order to please God, as in fact you are living. Now we ask you and urge you in the Lord Jesus to do this more and more."

Imagine how joyful Paul was to hear that these believers were standing firm and growing in their faith in spite of all they had encountered. He rejoiced that their lives had been transformed and that

they were serving the Lord. Paul wanted to encourage them to continue to grow spiritually, to continue to be transformed by the power
of God. This reminds me of what Paul wrote to the Corinthians
describing the transformation in their lives in 1 Corinthians 6:9–11:

> Or do you not know that wrongdoers will not inherit
> the kingdom of God? Do not be deceived: Neither the
> sexually immoral nor idolaters nor adulterers nor men
> who have sex with men nor thieves nor the greedy nor
> drunkards nor slanderers nor swindlers will inherit the
> kingdom of God. And that is what some of you were. But
> you were washed, you were sanctified, you were justified
> in the name of the Lord Jesus Christ and by the Spirit of
> our God.

Such were some of you until transformation came! Others
noticed the difference in their lives, and it is the same today as this
transformation works itself out in our lives. Our entire lives have
changed due to our sanctification and justification in the name of
Jesus and, as a result, our actions and attitudes change and continue
to change as we are transformed by the power of God.

Paul, being practical, then goes on in chapters 4 and 5 to recap for
the Thessalonians some of the instructions he had given to them and
encourages them to live out the transformation they have experienced
in Christ in order to please God and to serve him more and more.

Paul writes to them about ways of serving God through their
transformation in at least three areas:

1. in their personal lives: sexual purity, self-control, living a
   holy life, loving, being alert as children of light;
2. in relationships: loving others, building each other up, living
   in peace, helping the weak;
3. in their attitudes: being patient, joyful, prayerful, and
   thankful.

Because love is so crucial to each of these areas, Paul actually
talks about it a little more in depth when he encourages them to love
others more and more in 4:9,10:

> Now about your love for one another we do not need to
> write to you, for you yourselves have been taught by God
> to love each other. And in fact, you do love all of God's
> family throughout Macedonia. Yet we urge you, brothers
> and sisters, to do so more and more.

They weren't to be content in how they loved others nor happy with the status quo; they were to love others more and more. Peter also talked about this in his first epistle; 1 Peter 1:22 says, "Now that you have purified yourselves by obeying the truth so that you have sincere *love* for each other, *love* one another *deeply*, from the heart" (emphasis added). He recognized their transformation and their sincere love for others. He says to love, but then goes on to encourage them to love deeply. This love is what transforms us, and it is what should prompt the labor we do if we really want to honor God—it's probably what has to prompt this labor. This is the love we experience from God, and as a result we are channels of that love to others.

It is this unconditional *agape* love that prompts us to toil, to labor so intensely that the word itself produces the image of someone beating their breast as they labor with sorrow and troubles. Sacrifice is implied in this labor.

You know what it is like to be living for God, serving him in less than ideal circumstances. We miss our families and live among people who may not even want us there. We may lead people to Christ who will then experience worse troubles and lose more than we do. If single, you may be living in a place with fewer available single men, and letting go of that dream to be married is painful. You may be married and due to ministry constraints you feel like you cannot possibly keep up with all there is to do to maintain ministry to your family and to your community. There is overwhelming poverty, more needs than you could meet in a dozen lifetimes. You keep going, keep giving, keep sharing your faith, sometimes not seeing the results you had expected. Yet you continue to labor— because of the love you have received from God.

I think one problem we may encounter is that it is easy to forget what should be prompting our labor, because life and ministry are hard and we invest a lot of time and energy. We grow tired. Love may start to wane. And after a while it might not be love that is the motivation behind our labor. Let's take a few minutes to think about what could motivate our labor if we aren't motivated by love and what the outcomes of the different motivations would be.

If we continue to labor—to work really hard—and love isn't what is prompting us anymore, it could be that we are being driven by the desire to succeed, and so we keep working harder and harder, always striving to achieve the results we want. No one wants to fail in ministry. After all, people are giving and praying so that we can serve the Lord across cultures. So we continue to labor, committed to get the results that we want. Sometimes we just keep working, but soon we may have to fake the loving motivation—we can act like we love others, but inside we may actually dislike them. But to show dislike for someone is so unspiritual that we try to hide our attitude and keep acting. Sometimes we might deserve Oscars for how well we act. But how long can a person act without becoming exhausted?

We could also be motivated by guilt: Who will do this work if I don't? What would God do without me on his team? Though we grow so very tired, we have to keep working don't we? What happens if we rest or take a vacation? What will happen to the work? Sometimes it seems that we see this work as ours and we take on God's role. We forget what our role is supposed to be because we're too busy feeling discouraged that we can't work like God! We wonder what will people say if they ask how we are doing and we don't say we are very busy. Doesn't how busy we are equal how spiritual we are? We can become guilt ridden and duty driven, and our labor becomes even more of a hardship.

What would happen if another worker asked how you are and you said, "Fine, I just took a nap!" Ahh. Do workers take naps when there is so much to be done? Eternal destinations are at stake and we have to stay busy! What would people say if we are not super busy?

Being busy doesn't equal being spiritual. Johnny Miller, former president of Columbia International University, has said that sometimes it is spiritual to take a nap! When pride or guilt is our motivation, we will have a harder time taking a rest because we think we are indispensable! We are not.

So what happens when love isn't our motivation for laboring so intensely and these other motivations drive us? The results of working when love isn't our motivation, when it isn't what is prompting us to labor, can be a judgmental attitude or a heart of bitterness.

When others don't seem to be working as hard as we are, we can become judgmental. We can be legalistic in determining what is necessary and what isn't from ourselves and from others. Rather than criticizing each other, we should be each other's greatest encouragers and fans. It seems, though, that often we are critical of those who don't work as much as us. Pride can grow in our hearts, making us harsh with what we perceive as others' weaknesses.

On the other hand, it is also possible to become envious of those who seem to be able to do more than us. We may start to dislike them because we feel inferior. Comparing ourselves with each other is one of the most dangerous things we can do as women working across cultures. We all have different gifts; we are in different seasons of life; we have different energy levels; we were made to complete each other, not compete with each other. I am often tempted to wish I had others' gifts. When I hear someone effectively speaking to a large group, I find myself wishing that could be me. Or when I meet someone with an amazing ministry or exciting opportunities, I feel jealous. One thing I have started practicing that has been effective in battling these awful feelings of jealousy is that when I start to feel envious of others' gifts I stop and recognize that what I am doing is wrong. I then proceed to thank God for those gifts and ask God to bless their ministries and give them fruit. What starts out as whining ends up as seeking God's glory above all else. The focus is off of me and onto God. I thank him for the ministries of others and feel content with what God has called me to do. God put us in the body of Christ so that we could all work together for his glory.

I think, though, that the major effect of serving without love as our motivation is that we grow tired and ministry becomes self-generated and self-motivated. A result of that fatigue is that we are more tempted to give up as we can't live up to our expectations of ourselves. We can become so focused on ourselves that we think less about the Lord. Our will becomes supreme. These tiny seeds of selfishness that we all have are watered and fertilized; they start to grow, roots deepen, and the buds of selfishness blossom into full flowers of absorbing self-centeredness.

It comes back to whether we are living according to the flesh or whether the fruit of the Spirit is evident in our lives. God is the one who inspires us to labor with love, joy, peace, patience, kindness, goodness, faithfulness, gentleness, and self-control. When *agape*, this unconditional love, is what prompts us to labor, not only is how we view the labor different, but the outcomes of our labor are different.

A struggling church was looking for a new pastor and there was a tension in the atmosphere. They had an experienced pastor come as candidate. He preached and then attended a question-and-answer time with the congregation. One person stood up and asked him what he would do to bring healing and help to the church. His response was something like, "I will love on you." And in time, with that love, the church changed. I'm sure there were more difficulties, discussions, and issues to deal with, but everyone knew that this man loved them. One could feel it and see it. This pastor kind of oozed it in how he cared for people. The congregation grew as people loved more and more. The atmosphere became lighter, sweeter, and fuller. There was a unity that had been absent. Love transformed the church.

There is something about knowing we are loved that transforms us. We are encouraged.

Love transforms lives—both our own and others'—and almost always involves sacrifice. When my oldest son went to ask permission from his girlfriend's father to marry her, her father said if he could answer one question correctly he would give his blessing. The question was, "How would you define love in one word?" My son said he thought about it and said it was really hard to put love into one word. He finally decided on the word and looking her father in the eyes he said, "Sacrifice." With tears in his eyes her father said that was the exact word he was thinking of and promptly gave his permission.

After hearing this story I praised God for my son's insight . . . not just so he could marry Emily, but because he saw the connection between love and sacrifice.

With unconditional love as the motivation behind our labor, no matter how difficult it is, we can continue to labor. We expect to sacrifice, but we do so knowing we are loved. We are then empowered by this amazing love to labor.

Think about your team. Even when relationships are strong, Paul exhorts us to love more and more. However, we know there are times when we don't get along with our teammates, feelings are hurt, and expectations are not met. There are confrontations, boring team meetings, heated discussions about finances and vision that aren't fully aligned. How can our love for each other grow when sometimes we may not even like each other?

What about your national friends? Before we arrived overseas, I loved all the people we were going to minister among. Then we were lied to, stared at, robbed, and cheated. I was propositioned and harassed. My love for nationals didn't always come shining through. How does it feel when they disappoint you in how they treat you or are your friends only to see if you can help get them a green card? How can we grow in our love for them when at times we are tempted to stay inside our homes rather than face such different cultural norms? This unconditional love from God, which we've experienced firsthand and undeservedly, often transforms us most in the arena of sacrifice. Let me repeat that: this unconditional love from God, which we've experienced firsthand and undeservedly, often transforms us most in the arena of sacrifice. It is when we love others who do not deserve it that we show that we know what true love is. As we have been loved and as we love others, we are transformed by that love. As we are transformed, we truly love others and we sacrifice for them. This results in continuing transformation. It seems to me that we cannot love without sacrifice.

Because love is crucial in relationships and because Jesus said that people would know we are his disciples by our love, I want to love others more. The question is how. How can I love others more, especially when it seems impossible because they seem unlovable? Let's go to Scripture to see what can make our love for others deepen. Jesus talks about this when he was invited to the home of a Pharisee. We are going to learn that in order to love much we have to recognize how much we've been forgiven. Read with me to Luke 7:36–50:

> When one of the Pharisees invited Jesus to have dinner with him, he went to the Pharisee's house and reclined at the table. A woman in that town who lived a sinful life learned that Jesus was eating at the Pharisee's house, so she came there with an alabaster jar of perfume. As she stood behind him at his feet weeping, she began to wet his feet with her tears. Then she wiped them with her hair, kissed them and poured perfume on them.
>
> When the Pharisee who had invited him saw this, he said to himself, "If this man were a prophet, he would know who is touching him and what kind of woman she is—that she is a sinner."
>
> Jesus answered him, "Simon, I have something to tell you."
>
> "Tell me, teacher," he said.
>
> "Two men owed money to a certain moneylender. One owed him five hundred denarii, and the other fifty. Neither of them had the money to pay him back, so he forgave the debts of both. Now which of them will love him more?"
>
> Simon replied, "I suppose the one who had the bigger debt forgiven."
>
> "You have judged correctly," Jesus said.
>
> Then he turned toward the woman and said to Simon, "Do you see this woman? I came into your house. You did not

give me any water for my feet, but she wet my feet with
her tears and wiped them with her hair. You did not give
me a kiss, but this woman, from the time I entered, has not
stopped kissing my feet. You did not put oil on my head, but
she has poured perfume on my feet. Therefore, I tell you, her
many sins have been forgiven—as her great love has shown.
But whoever has been forgiven little loves little."

Then Jesus said to her, "Your sins are forgiven."

The other guests began to say among themselves, "Who is
this who even forgives sins?"

Jesus said to the woman, "Your faith has saved you; go
in peace."

I am struck with what happened when this sinful woman comes
and is crying so much that her tears are wetting the feet of Jesus and
she uses her hair to wipe them. She then kisses his feet and pours
perfume on his feet. All the Pharisee could think of was her sinfulness and unworthiness. All she could think of was her sinfulness,
unworthiness, and need. All Jesus could think of was her repentant
and loving heart. He forgave her many sins and, as a result of the
forgiveness she received, she loved much.

He then tells a parable of the two men being forgiven their debt,
one for a lot and one for a little, and how that influenced how much
they loved their moneylender for forgiving them. Jesus then points
out all that the woman had done for him in contrast to what his host,
Simon, had done when he entered the house.

Simon didn't think he had done that much that needed to be
forgiven, so he loved little. She realized she had been forgiven much,
so she loved much. Jesus says, "But whoever has been forgiven little
loves little."

Who of us has been forgiven little? In our relationship with God
and with others we all need to be intentionally aware of how much
we've been forgiven. This will be the impetus for not only our love
for God, but our love for each other. Think about all of the times

you have let go of or disregarded what someone did to hurt you. You forgave them. And think about all the times others have forgiven you in the same way. Forgiveness is in constant demand in all relationships. When forgiveness doesn't happen, relationships suffer. Indeed they might not survive.

We are all in need of grace and forgiveness. I often take his grace for granted and forget that forgiveness was given to me and not earned by being good or trying hard!

I have a friend named Delores. Her background is very different from mine. She was heavily involved in drugs. She was a prostitute. She spent time in prison. It was in prison that she met Jesus and ended up being set free.

I met her for the first time a few years ago when I was speaking at her church. She came up to me and told me how she met Jesus and how he saved her life. She now helps lead the worship at church. If she has to work on Sunday morning, she will go early to take her tithe. She walks to church through any weather. Her Bible is now worn and she almost always has a word of testimony to say about what God is teaching her.

When I saw her last I asked her what God had been teaching her. She told me how God had been at work in her to not pass people by but to share with them about the Lord. It may be outside on the street corner near a store. It might be in her neighborhood or on her way to work. She sees people with needs and she says she cannot pass them by without telling them about the Lord. She loves them. She has to share Jesus with them.

Not too long ago we were in church together. She was sitting up front to the side as part of the worship team when a woman stood up to sing "Redeemer." (You may want to take a few minutes and listen to this song online as sung by Nicole C. Mullen before reading further!) I sat there and thought what a beautiful song it was. The words were amazing and the singer's heartfelt love for the Lord was evident. I was enjoying the song when I couldn't help but notice Delores. Watching her worship the Lord as she listened to this song was like witnessing a private moment of worship between her and her God. I almost felt like I was intruding, but I was so drawn to her response to God that my heart began to melt.

Delores was weeping. She was sobbing. She could not stop crying, and with tears pouring down her face she cried out the name of Jesus with unreserved thanksgiving. She stood with her arms raised because she could not get over it. Jesus was her redeemer. He had forgiven her shame. He had rescued her from prison and delivered her from evil. Her redeemer was alive.

My past may be different than hers, but my sin is the same. I was not in a physical prison, but I was imprisoned by my own fears and greed. I had not sold my body, but I had sold my soul. I did not do drugs, but I used other things to satisfy the desires of my heart. I was a liar and a thief. I feared man and not God. I sought to save myself by being good and at times had a heart that was haughty and proud. In arrogance I thought I didn't need God. I was destined for judgment. I was going to be eternally separated from my heavenly Father and thrown into the lake of hell. That is what I deserve.

But I, too, met Jesus. And he saved me.

I think Delores realizes she was forgiven much. She loves more. I want to change—I want my heart to love more. I want to love Jesus like she does. I don't want to be able to hear that song and have my heart stay numb. It should move me to tears as I recognize the cost of my redemption and my sin that caused my Savior to suffer so that I could receive forgiveness. Not only do I want to love God more, but this love must affect my relationships. I have been forgiven much; the more I realize how little I deserve the love of God and yet how much God loves me, the more I will love others, because we are *all* in desperate need of forgiveness. I cannot hold a grudge against another or give hatred a corner in my heart toward another person when I realize the love and forgiveness I have experienced from God.

It is this kind of love we experience from God—unconditional love—that prompts us to labor so intensely. This labor that we are talking about isn't easy: Paul experienced sorrow in relationships; he and Barnabas parted ways; he was thwarted in his desire to see people; he had to leave people suddenly; there were lots of good-byes, as well as physical punishments and trials. He wrote to the Corinthians about what he experienced in 2 Corinthians 4:8–11:

> We are hard pressed on every side, but not crushed; perplexed, but not in despair; persecuted, but not abandoned; struck down, but not destroyed. We always carry around in our body the death of Jesus, so that the life of Jesus may also be revealed in our body. For we who are alive are always being given over to death for Jesus' sake, so that his life may also be revealed in our mortal body.

Yet through all of this he continued to love deeply. One of the reasons he continued to love through his labor is that he never forgot how much he had been forgiven. He wrote to Timothy in 1 Timothy 1:15 and said, "Christ Jesus came into the world to save sinners— of whom I am the worst." He remembered being a blasphemer, a violent man, a persecutor of the church. He recognized all he had been forgiven of, and so he loved deeply. He was transformed by the love he experienced from God, and it affected his love for others and prompted him to labor intensely.

As we recognize the amazing forgiveness we've experienced, our love for our Savior and for others will deepen and our labor will flow from it.

Questions:
How are forgiveness and love connected?

Why can bitterness be a common problem in churches and in ministry?

Resource:
The Arbinger Institute, *The Anatomy of Peace: Resolving the Heart of Conflict* (San Francisco: Berrett-Koehler, 2006).

Endurance Inspired by Hope Entails Working and Waiting

When I was in high school I was praying for my parents' salvation as well as looking for opportunities to witness to them. I remember once when I was leaving the house to catch the school bus, I asked my mother when she was going to get saved. She responded she wasn't ready, and I said, "You know you don't have forever," and then ran out the door! Please note, this is probably not the best witnessing strategy!

As I learned about Jesus coming again, I was worried that he would come when I was at school and my parents would worry because they wouldn't know where I was. So I would leave my Bible open in my bedroom to 1 Thessalonians 4:15–18:

> According to the Lord's word, we tell you that we who are still alive, who are left until the coming of the Lord, will certainly not precede those who have fallen asleep. For the Lord himself will come down from heaven, with a loud command, with the voice of the archangel and with the trumpet call of God, and the dead in Christ will rise first. After that, we who are still alive and are left will be caught up together with them in the clouds to meet the Lord in the air. And so we will be with the Lord forever. Therefore encourage one another with these words.

That way, if Jesus came back and took me to heaven during school hours, my parents would read that and know where I was. I remember riding the bus and looking at the sky wondering if he would come that day. I was expecting him to come any time!

My attitude through the years about his coming has ranged
from "Oh, not yet!" to "Oh, please come now!" When I was looking
forward to an event, I would want Jesus to delay his coming. When
life seemed overwhelming, I was ready for him to come as soon as
possible! I recognize these attitudes aren't necessarily spiritually
mature ones, but they have been how I've approached thinking about
the return of Jesus to this world.

As we look at endurance inspired by hope, we are going to see
how the Thessalonians endured as they waited and hoped for Jesus to
come again. They knew their life on earth was only temporary and
that eternity with their Lord was awaiting them. However, endurance inspired by hope entails not only waiting for him to come, but
working as we wait.

I really like the meaning of the Greek word *hupomone* for
"endurance." It is defined as steadfast, constant, patient enduring.
According to the *New Testament Greek Lexicon*, a steadfast person
can be described as someone "who is not swerved from his deliber-
ate purpose and his loyalty to faith and piety by even the greatest
trials and sufferings" (http:// www.biblestudytools.com).

To be unswerving sounds so courageous, so hard! I think of
marathon runners and my heart cringes, because in my heart I am
convinced I could never run one. Well, I could start, but I don't think
I would last to the finish line.

What is it that enables a runner to keep going mile after mile?
Along the same lines, how can a cross-cultural worker keep working
during difficult times?

I'm sure all of us know of those who have followed Jesus in this
life only to lose jobs, family relationships, freedom, and even their
lives. And yet people continue to follow after him. How do they do
it? It's because they know that this life is in preparation for the life to
come. This is only the prelude, the appetizer if you will, to the real
thing . . . eternal life in heaven.

So how do you keep working day after day when there are the
annoyances of getting your visas renewed, standing in long lines at

the registration office, not having Reese's Peanut Butter Cups easily available (although peanut butter chocolate chapattis are OK in a pinch!), hot weather with no air conditioning and sporadic electricity? There are the major issues of living far from loved ones, facing daily stresses, evading ornery cows and rascally monkeys, ministry in the midst of opposition, and balancing all you have to do in a mere twenty-four hours.

We can try by sheer determination to hang on and keep working, but if we lose sight of the big picture we will be tempted to give up, go home, and call it quits. Have you felt like that in the last six months? Or maybe even in the last two weeks? Life is hard anyway; living in a cross-cultural setting makes it even tougher.

If we do manage to stay put and keep on in ministry, but we have the wrong motivation, we might grow apathetic. There can be so many needs to meet and so few workers that it seems what little we can do just isn't enough, and somehow along the way we can almost stop caring. A heart seems to hold only so much pain before it may begin to grow cold

Or if you are facing more challenges than normal and team dynamics are tough, it might be easy to become cynical. We work in places where it seems what little light our lives shine only exhibits the things of darkness even more. I remember some team meetings when we were discussing finances or strategies that tempers flared. There have been times when I've been so discouraged by people's responses and comments and when I even got tired of my own humanness, that I've wondered how God can stay committed to using human beings.

And there are times in the midst of ministry when I just want to go home and for everything to be normal again. I'd have a normal job, a normal house, a dog, a picket fence, and a neighborhood church. I wonder what it would be like to live a more normal life. And then I ask myself, "What is normal?" It is when I start feeling like this that I have to stop and think, "OK wait, what in the world am I doing here? Why did I even begin this work of faith and this labor of love that takes me so far from my comfort zone?"

It all comes back to one little word that has huge ramifications: hope. Paul is writing about endurance inspired by hope. Hope (*elpis* in Greek) is defined as expectation of good, being joyful and confident. Hope. The hope that we have as we wait and look for Jesus to come back, the hope we have that life here isn't all there is. Life in heaven is where we truly begin to live.

What do we do when we are trying to endure but are running low on hope? What do we do when it seems that as we look at life realistically we aren't sure what we are doing is making any difference at all? Since it is easy to lose hope, we can ask ourselves some questions that will help us see problem areas that keep us from being women of hope.

One question we can ask ourselves is, "Who we are trying to please?" Paul writes in 1 Thessalonians 2:3–6:

> For the appeal we make does not spring from error or
> impure motives, nor are we trying to trick you. On the
> contrary, we speak as those approved by God to be
> entrusted with the gospel. We are not trying to please
> people but God, who tests our hearts. You know we
> never used flattery, nor did we put on a mask to cover
> up greed—God is our witness. We were not looking for
> praise from people, not from you or anyone else.

I was born a people pleaser and I tried to be superwoman. I didn't discover until I was in my late thirties that I can't live like that! It's too hard and people are too different. It is impossible to please them all the time. I need to remember that I live to please God, not people. It is so easy to lose hope when we are busy trying to please people. When they're happy, we can feel positive and hopeful, but when they're not, we lose hope because we are so busy trying to do what we can to make them happy again. Seeking to please God should be our heart's desire. When we are pleasing him, it doesn't really matter in the long run whether people are happy or not! Paul knew that God was his ultimate judge, the one he needed to please. He wrote in Galatians 1:10, "For am I now seeking the favor of men, or of God? Or am I striving to please men? If I were still trying to please men, I would not be a bond-servant of Christ" (NASB).

I love that last sentence. If I were still trying to please men, I would not be a bond-servant of Christ. When we try to please people, we will lose hope. When we try to please God and live for him, we are filled with hope because we know his opinion is the only one that counts. He not only loves us no matter what, he even gives us the grace and strength to live for him!

Paul also knew what really mattered in life. Most things in this life will not last; they are temporary. He knew that only two things last beyond this life: the word of God and people's souls. So he focused his efforts on these two things. He showed this when he told the Thessalonians that they were his crown, his joy, his glory in 1 Thessalonians 2:17–20:

> But, brothers and sisters, when we were orphaned by being separated from you for a short time (in person, not in thought), out of our intense longing we made every effort to see you. For we wanted to come to you—certainly I, Paul, did, again and again—but Satan blocked our way. For what is our hope, our joy, or the crown in which we will glory in the presence of our Lord Jesus when he comes? Is it not you? Indeed, you are our glory and joy. (NIV 2011)

He was looking ahead to what his labor now would mean in eternity. Does that not give you hope—that one day when we see Jesus there will be people in heaven that we have influenced? You may be thinking, "Well not anyone I've witnessed to here. I've seen no visible, tangible fruit yet in my ministry." A friend of mine prayed for her brother's salvation for thirty-five years before he came to Christ. I am so thankful she didn't give up and stop praying! A young man from my high school days became a believer, but I didn't find out for twenty years. Stories abound of seeds that were planted and not until years later was fruit finally borne or known about. We look at the present and may think we are failing. We lose hope when we focus on the present and forget about what God might do in the future.

So the second question we can ask ourselves is, "On what time frame are we focusing?"

We must realize that though the results may not be immediate, it doesn't mean that they won't eventually come. God uses weak people, even when they think they fail. He can take what we give, use it, and work everything together so that he is glorified by our desire to make Jesus known.

You may feel discouraged. You may not be seeing immediate results. You may not even feel wanted. Yet you can serve faithfully, trusting God to work, because God uses what you do and what others do in his own timetable. We work with each other like links in a chain that eventually reaches from one end to the other. We keep sharing our faith; we try new strategies and make changes as we serve the Lord; we persevere in ministry because we have hope that God is at work.

To maintain hope we can't let our present overshadow the eternal. We have no idea how God is using today to shape eternity. We have to work. We have to wait. We have to keep our eyes on eternity and not on what is here on earth, that which is temporary. So we must ask ourselves yet another question, "On what is our mind set?" Paul wrote in 1 Thessalonians 3:11–13:

> Now may our God and Father himself and our Lord Jesus clear the way for us to come to you. May the Lord make your love increase and overflow for each other and for everyone else, just as ours does for you. May he strengthen your hearts so that you will be blameless and holy in the presence of our God and Father when our Lord Jesus comes with all his holy ones.

Paul points their attention to their source for love and strength, as well as to that future day when Jesus is coming back. If there's one thing we should know, it is that we have to live with our eyes focused on what is to come and not what is. Paul talks about this in Colossians 3:2 when he writes, "Set your minds on things above, not on earthly things." When Stephen was stoned he had his eyes on heaven; Luke tells us in Acts 7:54–60 that Stephen focused on Jesus, not the people who were stoning him. When the Hebrews were going through persecution, they were encouraged to fix their eyes on Jesus, the author and perfecter of their faith. Paul also wrote to the Romans in Romans 8:17,18:

> Now if we are children, then we are heirs—heirs of
> God and co-heirs with Christ, if indeed we share in his
> sufferings in order that we may also share in his glory. I
> consider that our present sufferings are not worth com-
> paring with the glory that will be revealed in us.

What is coming is so much better than what is in the here and now. It's like the lady who, before she died, told the pastor she wanted to be buried with a fork in her hand. The pastor asked why. She replied, "Remember at potlucks and dinners that you always saved your fork because you knew dessert was coming? I want people to be reminded that after I die I know the best is yet to come." The more we look up, the more we know to hope. The more we look down, the more we will lose hope. Honestly, though, when I am going through a trial, when my present is so awful it seems to demand all my attention, sometimes it is hard to focus on eternity. It is then I need to ask myself, am I looking up or down? When I keep looking down—at what is here, at what I can understand, at what I can do, and what I know—I start to worry and fear rather than looking up expectantly while working and waiting.

If I were to focus more on God from the beginning of trials I experience and not be so consumed with the things in this world, I would have a better perspective to wait on the Lord, to have hope in him rather than fear his will for me and hold on so tightly to the present. Because of looking down at only what I can see and feel, I lose sight of hope. I forget about the glory to come, so I may not live well. It is only as we keep our eyes on eternity that we know how to live in the present.

What also brings hope is recognizing who is at work. Paul writes in 5:23,24: "May God himself, the God of peace, sanctify you through and through. May your whole spirit, soul and body be kept blameless at the coming of our Lord Jesus Christ. The one who calls you is faithful, and he will do it." God is at work and he is faithful. We are not left on our own. We have to ask ourselves, "In whom is our hope?"

It is too easy to put God in a box, to forget he is all powerful and is at work in us and for us. The same power that raised Jesus from the dead is at work in us! And yet sometimes I think something is too hard for God. How far from the truth is that?

When we began raising support to minister across cultures, I had my doubts as to whether God would be able to provide. Shame on me! Through these twenty-five years of ministry, God has always met our needs. My eyes have to focus on him and not on the need of the moment. He is the master and provider of all my needs of every minute of every day.

Finally, to maintain hope we need to ask ourselves if we are living purposefully. Paul gives a list of instructions for life in chapter 4, and in chapter 5 he writes even more about living as sons of light. He also mentions again the coming of the Lord to encourage purposeful living. Knowing that how we live influences others and affects eternity gives us hope that the way we live serves a bigger purpose than what we know. Whether things are going well or we are going through a trial, we can live for the Lord and be confident that he is at work through everything . . . the good and the bad, the successes and failures. His purposes will not be thwarted, and his glory will reign.

I would imagine that during World War II it was difficult to imagine anything good coming from such destruction and hatred.

Yet there were those who knew that how they lived mattered because Jesus was coming back one day. So there were those who lived with purpose.

Corrie Ten Boom was one such person. We visited her home in the Netherlands where she and her family hid Jewish refugees. They were found out and sent to a concentration camp. However, in the house there's a poem about a tapestry that is hanging on the wall. When you look at the back of the tapestry, it is a jumble of threads with no observable pattern. It looks pretty messy. It makes you think that the person making it must not have known what they were doing.

Life Is But a Weaving

My life is but a weaving
Between my God and me.
I cannot choose the colors
He weaveth steadily.
Oft' times He weaveth sorrow;
And I in foolish pride
Forget He sees the upper
And I the underside.
Not 'til the loom is silent
And the shuttles cease to fly
Will God unroll the canvas
And reveal the reason why.
The dark threads are as needful
In the weaver's skillful hand
As the threads of gold and silver
In the pattern He has planned
He knows, He loves, He cares;
Nothing this truth can dim.
He gives the very best to those
Who leave the choice to Him. (Anonymous)

If you turn the tapestry over and look at the golden crown on the front, it is pretty obvious that the one who made the tapestry did know what she was doing.

It is the observer who had it wrong, because she was looking at
it from the wrong perspective. Looking at only one side, she is not
taking into account the knowledge and skill of the embroiderer, nor
trusting that each thread has a purpose, nor that the final product
will be beautiful.

God is at work throughout our lives as we work and wait. We can
endure through any and every circumstance because we are inspired
by this hope. We know that Jesus is coming back. We need to live
expectantly and encourage others to do so as well. One day we will
be home. Home has a special meaning for cross-cultural workers
who tend to feel like aliens wherever we live. We don't feel totally
comfortable in our host culture since we are foreigners. We no longer
feel totally comfortable in our home culture since we've changed
by living away from it and have worked to adapt to a different one.
But one day Jesus will take us to live with him forever, and we will
finally and completely feel totally at peace in our eternal home.

I remember on one furlough we were driving from Dallas, Texas,
to Akron, Ohio. We were going to see my parents, to the place where
I grew up. I was going home. After a few hours of driving, I began
feeling weird. I felt sick but not with a normal headache or stom-
achache. This was the beginning of a more long-term illness (with
strange symptoms) called cytomegalovirus. I remember thinking
that my arm felt numb; my legs felt like they were becoming unat-
tached to my body; my heart was pounding. I was very afraid. I had
never experienced this kind of illness before. Whenever I would feel
any of these weird symptoms, and fears would be on the rampage
in my mind, one thought gave me comfort. One thought helped me
stay calm and in the vehicle. One thought soothed my worried heart.
"You'll be home soon and everything will be OK." I was thinking of
being in my parent's home, the place where I was always cared for,
always loved. I would be safe there. And so, on the long drive home,
I kept my eyes focused on what was ahead. Home.

Now I wasn't thinking of heaven. I was thinking of my earthly
home, and it gave me comfort. How much more should thoughts of

our heavenly home bring us comfort as we go through all this world throws at us! My experience in the van is a picture of how it should be for us when we think of our heavenly home.

In our lives, as we face difficulties and experience trials, we should (like the Thessalonians) be waiting for Jesus to come back. He will take us to our true home. That is the only place we will ever be truly safe and truly home: our heavenly home with our Savior.

Whatever you are facing, you can face it with confidence and move forward with endurance inspired by hope. Look at how the Hebrews put this into practice when they faced their trials with hope in Hebrews 10:32–39:

> Remember those earlier days after you had received the light, when you endured in a great conflict full of suffering. Sometimes you were publicly exposed to insult and persecution; at other times you stood side by side with those who were so treated. You suffered along with those in prison and joyfully accepted the confiscation of your property, because you knew that you yourselves had better and lasting possessions. So do not throw away your confidence; it will be richly rewarded.
>
> You need to persevere so that when you have done the will of God, you will receive what he has promised. For,
>
> "In just a little while,
> he who is coming will come
> and will not delay."
>
> And,
>
> "But my righteous one will live by faith.
> And I take no pleasure
> in the one who shrinks back."
>
> But we do not belong to those who shrink back and are destroyed, but to those who have faith and are saved.

They knew they had a better and lasting possession. They would receive what was promised. Jesus is coming back. We have that hope.

If we don't have hope we will shrink back . . . we will only seek to play it safe. We will be afraid to work and forget who and what we are waiting for. We won't venture out of our comfort zones. We can't because we don't have hope—that expectation for God to be at work. We will only do what we think we can do and never take a risk, never take another step of faith. Life is too scary without hope.

We've looked at work produced by faith, labor prompted by love, and endurance inspired by hope. We can't play it safe . . . that requires no faith, no love, and no hope. We are women of faith, women who love, women who hope in our God who is at work in us and the world around us.

Remember, it is going to be OK. We will be home soon.

Questions:
How could hope or lack of hope influence your life on a daily basis?

How could hope or lack of it influence a cross-cultural worker's life?

Resource:
For radio programs on different topics, including emotional health, for cross-cultural workers: http://www.membercareradio.com.

VII
Relationships

Family, friends, and teammates all form different levels of community. Sometimes we can become closer to teammates than we are to our own family members who are back in the States.

The dull ache that we feel in our heart from missing family can sometimes become sharper after Skype conversations where we can see and talk but can't be near and touch.

There are many smiles when opportunities come to say hello and many tears when we have to say goodbye. We can be tempted to hold our hearts in check because of the pain of all the comings and goings, yet we weren't made to hold back. We were made to be in relationship with others and to feel connected to our families and as believers to the body of Christ.

The next few pages have some stories about team, church, and family relationships. There will probably always be issues to talk through and forgiveness offered and received. We will need to be ready to trust God for any hellos and goodbyes that might come our way, knowing that one day goodbyes will end and relationships will be perfect.

But until then we have to keep working hard, loving deeply, and forgiving often.

My Sister's Tale of Epic Heroism

My sister, Debbie Downey, is my hero. She has written this story of how she saved my life when neither of us knew how to swim:

It was a lazy Sunday afternoon in Alabama. Susan and I had just finished up a fun-filled afternoon. We had been at the lake all day splashing, playing, and floating in inner tubes. Susan and I climbed out of the lake at the pier and were walking up the pier to go to the car to meet Mom and Dad.

Suddenly, out of nowhere, a devilish whirlwind with red hair pushed Susan in the water—deep, dark, murky water. When our cousin pushed Susan, it was as if everything began to happen in slow motion. Susan catapulted gently into the water. I looked up and Mom and Dad were very far away, and I knew it was up to me to save Susan. No one else was there to do it—all my other relatives just stood there like statues. I quickly (even though it was in slow motion, I moved quickly) went over to the ladder at the end of the pier and looked down into the depths of the murky water—I could see Susan's curly locks floating lazily in the water. I went down the ladder to the last step and tried to reach her hair—alas I could not! I then jumped into the water holding on to the last rung of the ladder with one hand. With the other hand I reached down, down into the hazy, swirling water and grabbed a handful of long tresses. With one hand I pulled my sister up out of the water by the hair on her head. It seemed like it took me forever to pull her up—but when she finally emerged, she bobbed up like a cork in a bottle; I believe she even made the popping sound.

All I can say was that when I finally saw her head come up out of the water—well let's just say that was the gladdest that I had ever been to see her face (at least up to that point in our lives). I then pulled her over to the ladder, helped her get her feet in the rungs, gave her a little push up onto the pier, and then climbed out. I glared at my evil cousin, and I saw Susan shoot her a guilt-inducing glance. I hugged Susan and she wrapped her arms around me like strands of *al dente* spaghetti. I asked her if she was alright and she said she felt like she was going to vomit. Thank goodness she didn't because at that time of my life, if she would have barfed on me, that would have tested my sisterly devotion to its limit.

Susan and I quickly made our way to the car where our anxious parents waited. (At least Mom was anxious— Dad just looked like everything had been under control the whole time.) We got in the car—I remember feeling shaky and cold and for some reason I felt very scared, I think because I knew that my sister could have drowned. I would have lost her.

I remember thinking what an awesome responsibility I had felt toward my little sister, and from that moment I knew I always wanted to be there for her if she needed help. I wanted her to know if she was ever drowning and no one else could or would help, I would be there to grab her hair, pull her up, boost her up onto the pier, glare at the person who had caused the incident and, yes, now I would even be able to hold her head while she threw up.

Note: The "devilish whirlwind with red hair" was our much younger cousin who has since apologized at almost every family reunion! All is forgiven, dear cousin!

Questions:
How has God preserved your life for his purposes?

What is God's purpose for your local church? The global church?

Resources:
Patrick O. Cate, *Through God's Eyes: A Bible Study of God's Motivation for Missions*, rev. ed. (Pasadena: William Carey Library, 2012); and Marvin J. Newell, *Commissioned: What Jesus Wants You to Know as You Go* (Saint Charles, IL: ChurchSmart Resources, 2010), http://www.churchsmart.com.

From Hot Pants
to Hot Flashes

I grew up at Chapel Hill Church. It was there I trusted Christ as
my Savior, was challenged to grow in my walk with the Lord, and
was given opportunities to serve. At the altar I had frequent times
of surrendering my life, confessing sin, and committing to follow
Jesus wherever he would lead. I had godly role models, amazing
youth leaders, and Sunday school teachers who invested in my life.
Mrs. Franke was one of my teachers. Mrs. Foraker was my pal in a
program at our church. Carol invited me to her house to go through a
discipleship book. I would come up with lists of questions and Pastor
Frank would provide answers. Uncle Bob gave me opportunities,
support, and freedom to practice and develop leadership skills. Mrs.
Wilson and Barb Hess were godly women who were my mentors and
showed me what it was like to be a woman who loved God and his
word. Mrs. Parker encouraged me to memorize God's word for Bible
quizzing and showed me how to keep following Jesus even when life
doesn't turn out as expected. Cross-cultural workers came regularly
to share what God was doing around the world.

I learned there that God answers prayer. As a young believer I
prayed for a new Bible during a youth group meeting. Several weeks
later an envelope was given to me containing enough money to buy
a new Bible. Wow. To this day I have no idea who gave that to me.
I searched through a catalog until I found just the Bible I wanted.
It had wide margins so I could take notes and write questions or
insights. I ordered it, and a short while later it was delivered to my
house. It was in a large box, and when I opened it I realized that I
had forgotten to read the small print in the catalog that said what size

it was. This Bible was more like a family Bible that you would place on a table or desk. It was pretty heavy to carry around. But that was God's answer to my prayer, and so I carried it to school, church, and Bible studies. It provided a lot of opportunities for witnessing since it was bigger than several of my high school textbooks combined!

I was taught to give by example and exhortation. I remember during church one of the pastors was praying for the offering they were about to collect. It seemed a rather long prayer and the words struck me. I looked at the person sitting next to me and said, "He makes it sound like it's a privilege to give." My friend said, "It is." Another lesson learned!

In high school kids would ask me what kind of church I went to. I didn't know what to say except that it taught the Bible. They pushed me for more details. Maybe they thought it was the church of big Bibles! I cornered one of the elders and asked him what kind of church it was. He told me it was a Christian and Missionary Alliance church. So the next time someone at school asked me what kind of church it was, I could tell them it was a C&MA church. They said, "So what kind of a church is that?" I replied, "One that teaches the Bible."

One of the things I never doubted was my love and acceptance there. No matter what. Growing up I went through several phases. No makeup. Too much makeup. Short dresses. Long dresses. Hot pants (I still can't believe I wore those to church!). My church family continued to love me.

About forty years have passed since those hot-pants days. I've gone through lots of phases since then—newlywed, young mother, tired mother, and grandmother. Through them all my church family has loved and supported me. They have loved me from hot pants through hot flashes; from miniskirts through menopause! Their love and faithfulness have greatly influenced my life and given me a solid foundation from which to serve, no matter what phase of life I'm in!

Questions:
What have you appreciated about your church family?

What would be some of the challenges for people planting churches in areas of the world that have been historically resistant to the gospel?

Resource:
J. Dudley Woodberry, ed., *From Seed to Fruit: Global Trends, Fruitful Practices, and Emerging Issues among Muslims*, 2nd ed. (Pasadena: William Carey Library, 2011).

Night Owl or Early Bird

While visiting the country we were hoping to call home, we stayed for several months with friends. You know how there are those who like to stay up late and those who like to get up early? When asked if I was a night owl or early riser when our kids were little, my husband and I decided that I was neither a night owl nor an early bird—I just had a few peak hours in the afternoon!

However, in comparison to Pearl, the friend who was hosting us, I am a night owl. One night one of my favorite movies of all time was on, but it didn't start until 11:00 p.m. I asked Pearl, who hadn't seen the movie, to stay up with me to watch it. She refused. I thought she would enjoy the movie, plus I really wanted to see it again but didn't necessarily want to stay up by myself. Thus I began my persuasive strategy to get her to stay up with me.

"So, we can eat popcorn and have a slumber party. Our husbands will be sleeping and we can enjoy the movie!"

"We can already be in our pajamas so that as soon as the movie is over we can go to bed."

"It will be fun!"

"Come on, you will love the movie!"

After some time I wore her down and she gave in, warning me that I might have to work hard to keep her awake.

Friday night came. It was great. We popped popcorn and snacked on it while watching a very adventurous movie. We chatted during commercials. She was doing great staying awake and we were both enjoying the movie.

It was almost 1:00 a.m. and the movie was almost over. There were ten minutes or so left. It was the climax of the movie—a chase scene with the good guy and the bad guy, both armed, on motorboats braving the high seas in the midst of a horrific storm. Would the good guy win? We watched with bated breath, almost on the edges of our seats.

The cable went out.

Pearl looked at me and I looked at her. We tried several channels and came back to the movie channel hoping against hope that it would come back on. It didn't. She made me tell her how the movie ended, and I did my best to make it sound as exciting as it was.

I must have failed because she said she would never stay up late to watch a movie again!

As teammates we are different. There can be members with high energy and low energy, introverts and extroverts, verbal processors and those who think without saying a word . . . people who stay up late and those who don't!

Pearl and I are different. She is an adventurous cook and can make anything taste good. She introduced me, who can be rather averse to trying new foods, to some amazing dishes by just encouraging me to try them!

She gave, I gave. We both tried new things, and we not only enjoyed the experiences but grew to appreciate each other more as well.

It will be fun to see if I can get her to stay up late again . . . and I hope she's coming up with a recipe for me to try!

Questions:

What can teammates who are so different do to promote unity in the midst of their diversity?

What can church members and/or teammates who are so different do to promote unity in the midst of their diversity?

Resource:

Duane Elmer, *Cross-cultural Servanthood: Serving the World in Christlike Humility* (Downers Grove, IL: InterVarsity, 2006).

Love Is Blind

When I was in sixth grade I was walking to school on the last day
before our winter break. There was a slight coating of ice and snow
all around me. Munching on my log pretzel as I walked, I was
thinking about Peggy Fleming, a figure skater I had seen, and her
performance. Appreciating that I was on the smoothest sidewalk on
our block, I felt inspired to try one of her moves. Next thing I knew
I had fallen to the ground and was trying to get up and run back to
my mom. I had broken my front tooth. She encouraged me to go to
school and not worry about it; we'd go see the dentist later.

Fast forward about ten years. After years of temporary caps, no
caps, treatments, and finally a permanent cap, I had become somewhat insecure about my teeth. Don and I hadn't been married long
and decided to go out to eat at a local fish restaurant. After thanking God for the food, we began to eat. I took one bite and realized
my cap had broken and fallen off. Startled, I covered my mouth
and began to cry. My husband looked confused at my behavior.
(This wasn't the first time or the last!) He gently asked me what was
wrong. I couldn't seem to answer. "Let me see," he said. I told him
that I didn't want him to see me like this. He wanted to make sure
there was no blood. I was too upset and kept my face hidden under
my hands as I sobbed. I finally managed, after much coaxing, to tell
him that my cap had fallen off.

He convinced me to let him see my mouth. "It doesn't look so
bad," he said. Pacified, I stopped crying and even found my cap in
my French fries. I went to the restroom to look in the mirror. In one
glance I went from being mollified to being horrified! I didn't know
they had filed the remaining tooth so far down and that after the root

canal it would have turned so black. Where my tooth should have been was a small, black stub. How could Don have said it didn't look so bad?

I returned to the table but was unable to eat. We left soon afterwards and I called the dentist to make an appointment. Bless his heart; the dentist fit me in the very next morning. Taking my cap with me, I sat in the office, not really opening my mouth until I was sitting in the dental chair. After looking in my mouth, he said he could make a new cap (a better one!) and could fix my old one to stay on until then. He patted my shoulder to comfort me and said, "Don't worry. I won't make you go out in public like that."

The dentist saw the ugly black stub.

My husband looked beyond the stub. He determined to only see the woman he loved.

There is great security and joy in knowing you are loved by someone unconditionally. It makes me want to smile—black stub, new cap, and all.

Questions:
What are the effects of showing unconditional love to others?

What could be some obstacles to showing unconditional love to others from a different culture?

Resource:
Francis Chan, *Crazy Love: Overwhelmed by a Relentless God*, with Danae Yankoski (Colorado Springs: Cook, 2008).

The Pedicure from Hel . . . Well, I Mean Not a Good Place

A friend invited me to a salon and said I could get a body massage, a facial, or a pedicure. It was her gift to me. I was touched by her thoughtfulness. I happily decided on a pedicure. I don't have them often, but when I do, they feel so good! You stick your feet in hot, scented, bubbly water, and your feet are massaged with aromatic lotions. The person works wonders scrubbing the dead skin off and making the skin underneath soft and smooth. After polishing your toenails, your feet feel and look like new! So I went with my friend. She mentioned it was not exactly the same as in my home country—more of a European style maybe? No problem, I thought.

At first all went well. There was the hot, bubbly water, and as I stuck my feet into the pail I sat back to relax. I saw several bottles of lotions and oils and relaxed even more. The relaxation pretty much ended when she began to trim my nails and clip away at dead skin. I'm pretty sure she clipped off a small part of my toes since I saw a bit of blood.

As she began to massage my feet, she went from using her hands to using her knuckles, digging them into my feet and pulling on my toes. Harsh and unaware (or uncaring) of my pain, she kept kneading. I was no longer relaxing. I was mentally reciting Psalm 23, focusing on verse 4, "Yea, though I walk through the shadow of the valley of death" (KJV). I thought this was going to be an example of no pain, no gain. So I endured, thinking that when it was over the result of feeling good then would be worth the agony now. However, as she pulled each one of my toes separately (I really do think they are a bit longer than they used to be), I began to doubt my wisdom and began praying, "Oh God! Let this end soon!"

I began to wonder if she was ex-military and was trained to use this type of pedicure to torture prisoners. Or maybe she didn't like Americans and she was getting revenge at my home country by hurting one of its citizen's feet! I was certain she had a secret agenda that included inflicting misery and torment.

I was loath to give her my other foot, but I did. The torture continued. I hadn't dwelt on Psalm 23 that much since my root canal! She kneaded and dug into my other foot, and then came what she did to my toes. She seemed to pull until she heard a slight popping sound from each one. My toes were not made to pop!

My prayer life was drastically escalating. I had never longed more for the return of Jesus to this earth! I was on the edge of my seat. Surely she sensed my discomfort. Well, obviously not, since she continued. Why didn't I tell her to stop? Why did I just sit there? Surely the end result would be worth the anguish!

Finally, after it was all over, I was released. The torture was over. I hobbled out of the room remembering to thank God that I hadn't chosen a body massage!

Questions:
How has God used pain in your life to help you gain insight into his plan for you?

How does God use pain and sorrow to build up his church and fulfill the Great Commission?

Resource:
Jill Briscoe, *Faith Enough to Finish* (Oxford: Monarch Books, 2001).

Tricky Team Relationships

Our team was having Communion. Time was allotted for anyone with a grievance to ask for or receive forgiveness so that relationships were intact before taking Communion. I remember sitting there with my eyes closed, so thankful that all my relationships were good.

I felt a tap on my arm. Sandy wanted to talk with me. I was shocked as she told me that I hadn't been the support she had needed, and she wanted to talk with me about it. I wanted to defend myself and tell her that she seemed so self-reliant that I didn't think she needed my help. However, I needed to ask for forgiveness for not reaching out as much as I should have. Forgiveness was sweet and communication restored. We were able to have Communion with no issue between us.

Team relationships are tricky. In churches in our home country, if we don't get along with someone or if there is a disagreement, it is no problem. We can move on to other friendships or switch churches. However, often on a team we are it—family, friends, coworkers— and there isn't really any other place to go.

We work through issues many believers don't get the opportunity or privilege to work through together. We lovingly butt into each other's lives. At times it isn't appreciated in the moment; usually after the passing of time it is.

I remember loving a coworker enough to talk with her about some concerns I had about her marriage. We loved some gals on our team so much that we asked questions about who they were dating. Gently, firmly, and tearfully we intervened and asked one dear friend to take some time to reconsider a possible engagement. We walked with another friend through a decision to stop dating a young man.

We encouraged relationships and helped facilitate engagements and weddings. Opportunities came our way to shelter young women from unwanted attention of unbelievers under the protective umbrella of our family. Our teammates, in return, loved us and our children enough to also lovingly confront us at times. Though it was difficult, we were grateful.

At times team relationships were strained. Voices were raised and tears flowed. At other times fellowship was sweet and we were like family for each other through extremely difficult times. Meals, prayers, visits, and advice were all offered in charity and a sincere desire to be a blessing.

After one particularly difficult morning as a young mother involving a child and a pair of scissors, I was at a loss and didn't know what to do. After dropping the kids off at school I went to a teammate's apartment. I didn't call to ask if I could come so early. I just had to talk to someone. She opened the door, and though still in her robe and a busy young mother herself, she took time to listen, comfort, and pray for me.

To my children these team members are their "aunts" and "uncles," though we are no longer a team and all serve on different continents. These dear "relatives" have loved, babysat, played with, and prayed for my children. They were role models so that my kids could see what loving Jesus as a young adult looked like.

When one of my kids graduated from high school, she got a congratulations card from Aunt Molly. When she opened it up, a check fell out. She let the check lay on the ground where it fell as she eagerly looked at the photo Molly had enclosed. It was a picture of her with our daughter when they were both a lot younger! Kristi squealed, "Look at this picture! It's from Aunt Molly!" She appreci-ated the graduation gift, but the gift of having Molly as her aunt was even more prized!

Questions:

How do you know when to confront teammates and when to stay silent?

How does culture influence relationships and leadership?

Resource:

James E. Plueddemann, *Leading across Cultures: Effective Ministry and Mission in the Global Church* (Downers Grove, IL: IVP Academic, 2009).

Ode to Samson

Samson had long hair. That's about the only thing our dog Samson had in common with the Samson you read about in the Bible. Well I guess they both caused a lot of destruction too! Our Samson was part Pomeranian and part Chihuahua. Living with Samson was like living with a toddler in the terrible twos for about eight years!

We weren't supposed to have a dog. My husband grew up taking care of a pony, and I guess cleaning up after one of those alters your opinion on having pets. Nevertheless Katie, our youngest daughter, wanted a dog. Her dad said no. As I was tucking her into bed one night, she had a bright idea, "Can I pray about getting a dog?" I assured her she could but told her to keep in mind that God doesn't always give us what we want. Within days, without knowing she was praying, my husband had reconsidered the dog idea. "It's not really fair for me to say no dog. Just keep in mind that he won't be my responsibility. He'll be yours and the kids'."

This was just days before Katie's birthday, so off I went to the dog pound to see what I could find. There was Samson—a cute, energetic, little red-haired puppy. We surprised Katie with Samson for her birthday.

My husband was wise to not take responsibility—house training, feeding, taking him for walks all combined to fill quite the list of chores! Samson could sit when he wanted, speak without anyone asking him to, and go into his crate when bribed. He stole things from guests' purses, and when he got hold of candy he turned vicious if you tried to take it away. He could run like the wind, which he did as often as he could escape from the house. As much as he was outside, one would think he would take care of all his bodily functions while he was out there. No, Samson had frequent accidents, and sometimes he just did it on purpose for the attention, I guess.

He bit a woman who was staying with our kids (he found some candy in someone's purse and turned defiant to protect his loot). His incessant bark riled a neighbor who wrote us an anonymous note: "The neighborhood used to be quiet until you moved in." He stole my daughter-in-law's inhaler and, though we eventually got it from him, I'm sure it was quite gross!

After about eight years I noticed he was losing weight and didn't seem quite normal (I mean less normal than what was normal for him). I took him to the vet. After running some tests it was determined that Samson had kidney disease. There was no cure. However, expensive treatments were available to prolong his life for some time. We didn't have the money to do that and help our kids with college expenses, so we had a tough decision to make.

Don and Katie told me to decide, and so one morning I took Samson to the "surrender" side of the dog pound. It's a really nice sign, and they are trying to make it sound like a good thing, but really I was taking Samson to his death and it hurt. As naughty as he had been, he had still been a part of our family for eight years, and I cried as I handed him over to be surrendered.

Don was concerned about the timing. He said that I didn't waste much time between the diagnosis and the surrender. He wondered what my quick action would mean for him . . . so he said that if he ever had a kidney problem he wasn't going to tell me!

Questions:
What are life lessons we can learn from "difficult" pets?

What is a believer's responsibility in caring for God's creation?

Resource:
Eden Vigil is a ministry committed to environmental missions: http://edenvigil.org.

VIII
A Deeper Look at
Hope and Security
in God Alone

There are always relationship challenges. Whether we are single or married, young or old, urban or rural, unless we live on a deserted island we will relate to others, and as a result we will face conflict.

Conflict affects us most when we depend on others for what only God can give. If we look to others for approval, they may give it sometimes or withhold it, but they often don't know the full picture to determine whether to give it or not. Or they may give it but it is so subtle we don't even recognize it when it comes!

Relationship challenges also seem to increase when there is increased fruitfulness. Several have come to faith and a cell church begins. There is great excitement, and then a leader makes a decision without consulting the team. A team member begins dating someone from the host culture who is probably not a believer. A couple separates. Finances are tight. Heated arguments escalate and from the outside looking in it is hard to tell that the team is made up of mature believers who love each other. Spiritual battles rage as the team seeks to realign itself with the will of God and with love for each other.

Family emergencies back in our home country occur and we feel guilty we aren't consistently there to be of help. It puts a strain on already tenuous family relationships with those who aren't entirely convinced we are where we should be. After all, there are nonbelievers back home.

Churches split, support decreases, and before you know it you are undersupported. People get sick, someone is confronted, and we aren't taking the time we need to examine ourselves before scrutinizing anyone else. Soon all these varying ingredients combine, resulting in repeatedly rupturing relationships. Stress affects relationships. Relationships affect attrition. Attrition affects the spread of the gospel.

When we take the time to examine ourselves before inspecting anyone else, relationships are better. When we keep short accounts and forgive as Christ forgave us, relationships can flourish.

When we recognize that we must first look to God for all things, relationships are healthier. When we look to ourselves, idols, or anything other than God, relationships suffer. There are two stories in the Old Testament that show us this. We will take a look at Micah and Jonah and see what they teach us about ourselves and God.

We will see that life itself is really not all that much about us or for us; it is about God and for God. God alone.

"What Else Do I Have?" (Micah)

I had never heard of Divali before, but we just finished our second year of fireworks, lights, and neighborhood celebrations of this Hindu holiday. These celebrations seem to focus on wealth, good winning over evil, and new beginnings. I'm not sure how the fireworks fit in, but people save all year for the opportunity to participate in setting them off, the bigger and louder the better! Men and women fill temples with offerings, and several young men deftly place their fire offerings on the side of the road.

We were invited to our neighbor's house for dinner, and there we ate with a very large, elegantly framed picture of the elephant god Ganesh looking down at us as we ate. We've been inside a temple dedicated to monkeys, and monkeys indeed rule that temple! They roam freely and are often combative when trying to get something they want from one of their worshipers or even innocent bystanders!

After seeing so many idols, I am becoming more sensitive to idolatry in my own life and wanting to worship only God. I hadn't really thought much about idols before moving to South Asia. I knew it was written in the Ten Commandments that we weren't to have idols, but that was about it. Because I didn't make a golden calf, I thought I was doing pretty well! I was very sheltered from the idolatry that exists around the world. I am sheltered no more.

Idolatry is the worship of idols. "Idol" is defined in several ways, including "an image or other material object representing a deity to which religious worship is addressed" and "an image of a deity other than God" (http://www.dictionary.com). I also think an idol is anything I want so much I feel like I have to protect it. And who am I trying to protect it from? God.

I don't know all the reasons why idolatry exists. People were made to worship. People want to have control, and it seems easier to try and manipulate the gods they make than to trust the One they cannot see and who cannot be manipulated. Pride plays a big part in that we think we have some semblance of control when we focus on manmade things. We imagine we can reach out and touch God by our own actions and words. It makes us feel small when we think of a being beyond our world who knows more and can do more than what makes us feel comfortable.

Time and again in the book of Judges we see the endless cycle of faith in God, turning away, suffering, and turning again to God. During this time there was also idol worship and, generally, whatever each person thought was right, she did. The first time I read about Micah in Judges 17–18, I was struck first of all by the actions of his mother and her encouragement of her son's idolatry and then ultimately by the emptiness of Micah's life due to his worship of and dependence on idols and his own brand of religion.

Micah's mom realized that 1,100 shekels were stolen from her, and she uttered a curse on the person who took them. This fear of her curse led Micah to realize that he needed to confess, and when I read this the first time I was really proud of Micah's mom at the beginning. She was going to forgive him and turn the curse into a blessing. She said, "I solemnly consecrate my silver to the Lord" (17:3). When I read this I thought that was so cool . . . until I finished reading her sentence, "for my son to make an image overlaid with silver. I will give it back to you." She was consecrating her money to the Lord in order to make an idol. How could she even say two such opposing ideas in the same breath?

My pleasure in her response quickly turned to dread. She gave two hundred shekels to the local silversmith to make them into an idol so Micah could put them in his house and add them to his collection of gods.

So hold on a second. He stole 1,100 shekels. First, she said that she was going to dedicate her silver to the Lord to make an idol. This shows, yet again, the theme during the time of the judges: "Everyone did as they saw fit" (17:6). Secondly, she keeps the other nine hundred shekels for herself. I'm not sure how she sees this as consecrating her silver to the Lord! She encourages her son in his pursuit of idol worship, actively turning him away from the one true God.

One of the problems with idol worship is that idols can never be enough to satisfy a person's needy soul. Many idols are made with one particular purpose in mind—prosperity, life, fertility, and the list goes on. This could be why there are over 330 million gods in Hinduism!

We see Micah discontent with the idols he had, even with his new ones. He had a shrine and an ephod and even got one of his sons to be a priest. Then he met a Levite from Bethlehem and hired him to be his priest for ten shekels of silver per year as well as his food and clothes. So this young Levite priest started working for him, and Micah said, "Now I know that the Lord will be good to me, since this Levite has become my priest." He was coming to God on his own terms and seeking God's blessing in his own way. He wasn't concerned with God's law or how God had said to come to him. Micah developed his own way of approaching and pleasing God, seeking to earn his favor so his life would go well.

All was going smoothly until the Danites showed up. In Judges 18 the Danites stole Micah's gods and even took the priest away for their own use. Micah was devastated and gathered some men to go fight them in order to bring the gods and his priest back. But he was outnumbered and knew his men would be killed if they fought to protect his gods. When Micah realizes that he couldn't protect his gods or get his priest to return, he utters some of the saddest words I've ever read, "What else do I have?" (18:24). With that he turned around and went back home empty-hearted and empty-handed.

I guess this is what happens when we trust in idols. There is no security, and hope is merely an illusion. When we realize the futility of trying to protect our gods and that they cannot help or protect us, we recognize that we are left defenseless.

I can think of one idol in particular that has left me feeling unprotected and lacking. It is the idol of receiving the approval of others. When I could gain their approval, all was right with my world. When approval was withheld, I felt unwanted and doomed to failure. What else did I have when what I wanted and thought I needed was taken away? Living life joyfully while dependent on the approval of others is unattainable. We end up having to protect our gods rather than knowing our loving heavenly Father God is there to protect us when we trust in him. Living without him and only having idols keeps despair crouching at the door of our hearts.

There is also the idol of my own comfort and trying to do all I can to make sure my life is as uncomplicated as possible. There must be some connection to liking control over my circumstances. Again, this idol cannot meet my needs. I cannot meet my own needs.

If idols are all we have and they are taken away, what else do we have?

Let's contrast Micah's response in Judges 18:24 to Peter's response in John 6:68,69 when Jesus asked if his disciples were going to stop following him as others had done. People had stopped following Jesus because they didn't understand some of the harder things he was teaching them. They gave up and turned back. They left Jesus. So Jesus looks to his disciples and asks them if they would be leaving as well. "Simon Peter answered him, 'Lord, to whom shall we go? You have the words of eternal life. We have come to believe and to know that you are the Holy One of God.'"(NIV 1984)

What a world of difference in these two answers! Micah recognizes the emptiness of idol worship and is left with nothing. Peter recognizes the one true God and knows he need not go anywhere else. He knew the one true God, the source of eternal life!

There is only one God. Jesus is the one with words of eternal life. There is nowhere else to go. That is why we do what we do, why we move when he calls, and why we follow him wherever he leads. Even in dangerous circumstances we have our hope, peace, and security in Jesus Christ. He can never be taken away. He is always the victor.

There is a very big difference between Micah and us. Micah's hope was placed in a thing, a person, a place . . . something visible but temporal. He was left asking, "What else do I have?"

Our hope is in Jesus who is everywhere, knows everything, and promises to never leave us no matter what. We do not see him, but he is eternal. We contentedly ask, "What else do I need?"

Questions:
How has idolatry influenced you and the society in which you live?

How has idolatry influenced the society in which you live?

Resource:
Timothy Keller, *Counterfeit Gods: The Empty Promises of Money, Sex, and Power, and the Only Hope that Matters* (New York: Dutton, 2009).

Forfeiting Grace (Jonah)

I think one of the most striking sentences in Scripture is found in Jonah. From the belly of the great fish Jonah had time to ponder who he was, who God was, and what really mattered in life. He concluded, "Those who cling to worthless idols turn away from God's love for them" (2:8).

I remember a sermon illustration about a monkey that was put in a room with a large jar of special treats. There was one problem. The jar had a small opening. The monkey could put his hand in; however, when he filled it with treats he couldn't get it out. Had he grabbed just a little bit at a time, he could have eaten his fill over time. But he didn't see that. He only saw all that could be his if only it would come out in his hand. Left to his own desires the monkey would have sat there with one hand in the jar unable to do anything else but keep trying to get his handful out of the jar. He filled his hands with what he wanted, only to find that it wasn't working out the way he expected. However, that didn't change his approach, because he was selfishly focused only on what he wanted. When our hands cling to things that we want in this life, namely our idols, we don't have the capacity to grab hold of what we really need, God's love.

I've seen many different idols around the world. There are special trees that are given special honor. Hand-carved statues are made of all different materials and painted various colors. Some are beautiful and others are hideous. I've seen incense burned and floral offerings made to statues, both large and small, as people bow and back out of ornate temples. There are beautiful temples and holes in the wall where people go to worship. In my home country, idols seem to be less visible and more ideological. There are the pursuits of wealth, power, and prestige. Pleasure has become a god in much of the West, when nothing must come between us and what feels good, even if what feels good is wrong. We want what we want and we push God to the side. What is amazing is that God allows us to do that. Pushing God away is not new; it always happens when there is idolatry. Notice that when God was talking to Jeroboam through Ahijah the prophet in 1 Kings 14:8–10, he mentions how Jeroboam had turned his back on God due to the idols he had made:

> I tore the kingdom away from the house of David and
> gave it to you, but you have not been like my servant
> David, who kept my commands and followed me with all
> his heart, doing only what was right in my eyes. You have
> done more evil than all who lived before you. You have
> made for yourself other gods, idols made of metal; you
> have aroused my anger and turned your back on me.

Jonah also pushed God aside. He knew what God wanted him to do and where God wanted him to go. He decided to ignore God and run away from him—never a good idea! What idol made him choose to run? Maybe it was his own idea of what God should and shouldn't do; maybe it was his own comfort, which we see later in his story was important to him. Whatever it was, it became more important to him than obeying God.

He ends up on a boat going the wrong direction when a violent storm tosses the boat to and fro in the midst of the sea. Even the most experienced sailor was at a loss as to what to do in the midst of the storm. Nothing worked, and Jonah suggested they throw him overboard since it was his fault they were in the storm. There was an immediate calm after Jonah was tossed into the sea.

You know the story. God provided a great fish to swallow Jonah. Let's face it: there can't be much to do in the dark insides of a big fish! A person can do a lot of thinking when there isn't much else to do, and that is what Jonah did. He began to pray, remembering all that God had done for him and looking to his merciful God for help.

He recognized that God is patient and had protected his life so that he would have the chance to obey and serve the Lord with his life.

God often uses suffering to get our attention. It could be related to our own choices, as it was with Jonah, or it could just be a situation God divinely orchestrates so that we will recognize our dependence on any false idols and begin to rely solely on him once again.

When I take the time to examine my values, the things I cling to are often related to safety and security. What if I get on a plane and it crashes? What if our retirement fund isn't there anymore due to difficult economic times? Maybe if I just stay home I won't get hurt.

I remember visiting some friends in Delhi and them telling us about a shopping area within walking distance from their home. We wanted to get a few souvenirs to take back home, so we went to the stores and enjoyed looking at and purchasing a few things. After a short while I was ready to leave. Usually Don gives out before me when we're shopping, but I wasn't feeling all that great and was ready to go back to our friends' place. We arrived at their house, and within five or ten minutes people were calling to see if we were OK. It turns out that a bomb had exploded in that same shopping area just minutes after we had left it.

I am ill equipped to plan for my safety. I don't know enough and I am not powerful enough. I cannot make safety my idol or my major goal in life. Only God knows enough to take care of me, and he puts me where he knows it is best for me to be. Maybe one day it will be where a bomb will go off. I will leave that in his hands. I know that I have to seek him and not let anything else ensnare the desires of my heart.

Jonah discovered that truth after trying to go somewhere other than where God wanted him to be.

Usually our idols are those things we desire that are truly found only in God himself. We have idols when we try to find what we want apart from him and make them our goals rather than him.

Jonah eventually went where God told him to go and did what God told him to do. We read that, as a result of God's compassion toward Nineveh, Jonah was displeased with God, and we get a glimpse into what was in Jonah's heart when he ran the other direction away from God's will for him. He didn't follow God because, in Jonah's words, "I knew that you are a gracious and compassionate God, slow to anger and abounding in love, a God who relents from sending calamity" (4:2).

Wow! Those are reasons I would want to follow God—his graciousness, compassion, patience, and love! Unless, of course, those conflict with what I want to see happen. Jonah had a plan, and God was working out his own will in direct opposition to what Jonah thought was best.

And God gives Jonah a little object lesson. Jonah made himself a shelter and sat under it as protection from the sun. God made a vine to grow so that it would provide Jonah with even more shade to ease his discomfort. This made Jonah happy.

I can relate. On one of our trips in the heat of the summer to Varanasi, we were riding in a taxi. It was stifling hot, but a light breeze would come in through the window as the taxi progressed through traffic. It broke down three times. The first time we were in the sun. I began to sweat profusely. I had one small bottle of water, and I tried to drink it sparingly when I really wanted to just pour it over my head! Soon the taxi driver got it started again and off we went, only to break down a little further on our way, but this time it was under a tree. That tree made a huge difference in our comfort level! We were in the shade and, though it was hot, it was bearable. After we got going again, it broke down the third time, and that is when we changed taxis!

The shade of a tree made it so much more comfortable as we were out of direct sunlight. I can imagine how much more comfortable Jonah was under the vine. God also provided a worm to eat the vine and a scorching east wind so that when the sun blazed on Jonah's head he felt faint and wanted to die. He not only wanted to die because of being uncomfortable, he was also so angry that he thought life wasn't worth living. His enemies get to live though they deserved punishment; he deserved comfort (after all, he was obeying God now) and God had taken away what he had already given to make him comfortable.

God spoke clearly to Jonah about Jonah's attachment to this vine that he did nothing to cultivate. It was a gift of God, and yet the gift became the focus more so than God himself. God also points out that if Jonah could feel that way about a vine, how much more compassion should God feel for 120,000 people that he had made!

When worthless idols take the place of God, our priorities get screwed up. We lose sight of what is really important in life and ultimately forfeit the grace that could be ours.

As workers it can be easy to judge the idolatry that is around us without taking the time to evaluate where our hearts are. We may worship the image we seek to portray of a "successful" worker. We may have selfish motives and set ourselves up on the throne of our lives. Or we could worship the vision of God as we want him to be and not as he is, and when he takes away something that is precious to us we get angry and may even want to die—we are so disappointed in how life has turned out.

It is in these very moments of despair that God is seeking to speak to us as he did to Jonah in the belly of the whale. "Look to me," he says. We aren't to look to ourselves or to our circumstances to find contentment. We aren't to want our own will above his and run when his will doesn't coincide with ours.

The whole point of him being God is that he is the only being worthy of worship. Because this is true, he goes to great pains to show us the futility of idolatry. After some of the initial disappointments in life when God doesn't show up the way we thought he would or when we realize we have been trusting in something or someone other than him, we look to him and we find everything we've been searching for apart from him. He is all we need, our unmovable rock and eternal anchor in the midst of a worm-eaten world where nothing else lasts.

I find comfort in knowing he is God and that whenever I run, he will find me. I cannot hide. I cannot go so far that he isn't already there. What Jonah was complaining about, we can find great comfort in. Unlike Jonah, we recognize that we need all that God is, and when we come to him we appreciate the qualities that Jonah only associated negatively with how God would treat Jonah's enemies. Knowing we were God's enemies and that God still loved us and gave his only Son for us thrills our hearts and impels us to share this message, because we know that God is "a gracious and compassionate God, slow to anger and abounding in love, a God who relents from sending calamity" (Jonah 4:2).

May every tongue, tribe, and nation praise his worthy name!

Questions:
Have you ever felt like Jonah? If so, how did God work in your life?

What training is available for women as they serve across cultures that will help them finish strong and not react to God as Jonah did?

Resource:
Curriculum for women to use in training other women for a lifestyle of ministry: http://www.entrust4.org/about/our-ministries/wwmt/curriculum-samples.

References

Addington, T. J. 2010. *Live like you mean it: The 10 crucial questions that will help you clarify your purpose / live intentionally / make the most of the rest of your life.* Colorado Springs: NavPress.

Bridges, Erich, and Jerry Rankin. 2005. *Lives given, not taken: 21st century Southern Baptist martyrs.* Richmond, VA: International Mission Board.

Briscoe, Jill. 2001. *Faith enough to finish.* Oxford: Monarch Books.

Eenigenburg, Sue, and Robynn Bliss. 2010. *Expectations and burnout: Women surviving the Great Commission.* Pasadena: William Carey Library.

Hurst, Aggie. 1986. *Aggie: The inspiring story of a girl without a country.* Springfield, MO: Gospel Publishing House.

McGee, Robert S. 2003. *The search for significance.* Nashville: Thomas Nelson.

Walvoord, John, and Roy B. Zuck, eds.1988. *The Bible knowledge commentary.* Colorado Springs: Chariot Victor Books